THE

UNCONDITIONAL

★

A

LYRIC

Simon Jarvis

Barque 2005

PUBLISHED BY BARQUE PRESS
c/o Keston Sutherland & Andrea Brady
70a Cranwich Road, London N16 5JD, United Kingdom

www.barquepress.com
info@barquepress.com

All rights reserved

© Simon Jarvis 2005

The right of Simon Jarvis to be identified as the author of this work has been asserted by him in accordance with Section 77 of the Copyright, Designs and Patents Act 1988.

First published in 2005

Printed and bound in the United Kingdom by Antony Rowe Ltd

Typeset in Garamond 9.5pt

British Library Cataloguing-in-Publication Data

A catalogue record for this book is available from the British Library

ISBN 1-903488-43-5 hardback

The publisher gratefully acknowledges financial assistance
from Arts Council England

THE UNCONDITIONAL

To the Auditor

Nulle part, à cause des nuages, on ne distinguait le soleil ni aucun place bleue qui fît sourire le firmament; mais à un certain endroit du lac, sur une certaine zone indécise, on voyait, non pas l'image même du disque, pourtant une lumière blanche, éparse, réfléchie, de cet astre qu'on ne voyait pas.

Data float down; the own rote load doles out
        a doubt-loud flow into the overload.
Facts, moping at their blindless diurn, tread
        the light to dumb muck for cash in one line.
Hush dim glut making a linear red.
        Hush now to a mindless lucky smash.
Infinitesimally aperture
        the single seamless of the done told world
or prise the top off the creep in one dull.
        Now, last low vocative of the ending-cult,
blow out the pilot light.
        Disintermediate the vocoders.
Empty this plea of efficacity.

        A little arch; a grille of iron struts.

The Unconditional

A glass; opaque; a frosted top; a bar;
        these at the summit of the stairwell stood
looking like exit roads or looking like
        some vents for losses or for loss of loss
or looking forcibly like free redoubts
        lit with a promise of the best way out
or with true intimations of an end
        gripped =x's motor motors by the tip
of all the light dropping inside his lip
        as two steps forward lead to three more back
while the best impulse rushes into lack
        he recoiled from the newel-post to leap
running upstairs to push his willing teeth
        into and through the glass and to an air
hoped sung and stammered by what broke bones there
        suspended in brown vacancies of shade
crowding their varnish to a wooden glade
        of former trees whose long surrendered height
observed no alterations in the light
        as =x first climbed the stairs and then climbed down
backwards from Eden with no smile nor frown
        breaking the clench of composited teeth
incompetent to choose help or relief
        so his null feet just rattled up and back

The Unconditional

the gradus ab's drab retrogressive track
        painting with clatters wavers in his eye
which ever hovers over this goodbye
        whose yes yes, no, no no no no, then yes
makes one upright or disassembled mess
        when two steps backward and three stumbles up
leave his lip wobbling at the bitter cup.
        He stands or runs; he mounts, recedes; he sits.
He crawls; he clambers; gapes, ingests; he grips.
        He breathes or coughs; he sings or vomits; spits.
He stares or blinks; he leaps and bounds; or trips:
        Read it or do not read it, then regret
both what you did and what you did not yet
        as one shade greener on the other side
darkens amassing grasses it belies
        with indecisive umbers ever spread
on the true colours of the mortgaged head.
        He gasps, then giggles; he caresses, hits;
retires, revolts, reviles, repairs, remits.
        Dissolving slowly in this single dusk
he chokes, drinks, lowers, shines, goes out and just
        forgets to notice how this leap or lack
hummed through each lungful heaves up or drags back
        in every utterance of good or ill

The Unconditional

leaving him circling motionlessly still.
        At that long instant one face fell to earth.
Another rose up into joyless mirth.
        Only the human bit descends below.
The others take it as their part to go
        off like some protocols into the world
so inconspicuously chitinous
        as marine skeletons distributed
across this speaking singing face of print.
        He takes this moment for a crisis since
he folds away the quavers or the prints
        whose inky intonations mark this will
to some self murder or to some resolve
        not as the terminus to which he comes
but rather as his daily meat and drink
        which make up meaning in what he can think
as every impulse of his working brain
        is suicessionally caught in train
(lacking those questions which make up the real
        essential stuff of things and by whose force
a vocal avocet is set above
        a sky or pool which ripples with a blank
implenitudinable and still more
        an inannihilable sung contour

The Unconditional

holding the set of legal English tunes
        retained in carbons or on other moons
(since all those questions are that substantive
        essential content of the universe
prohibited in 1866
        by the academy of suicides
(while a sole instant which prepares suspends
        paints in pluperfect all that follows here:
all wrong detections of what outer things
        wish all deletions inside-out or sings
angelic and indelible one scale
        of more than adamantine questions' lit
(of more than adamantine since their ladder
        concludes invisible in air or madder
(and so the first hexameter declares
        the first word sung or spoken which prepares
the first thought and the first fuck and the first
        now pre-prohibited refreshed first thirst
unanswered undisanswerably live
        just as whoever would exchange must give
just as a motor coughs itself to life
        or just into what mechanism is
being what neither coughs nor coughs to life
        nor what can be ignited short of that

that is that overspill that has it live
        in every energy its death expends.
Just as a repetition starts with one.
        Just as a single lived experience dies
or just congeals into its brilliant idol
        whose smiling permanence afflicts the air
knowing it cannot ever learn decay
        or still diminish like an unmade thing
or like a screen which having learnt to think
        learns to forget the images it bears.
Just as a margin holds and frees its type
        or just sits blankling in the wasted space.
A dog returning to its vomit sings
        as much as these bones may be said to live
or bond the human something stuck inside
        their numbers told off every time they come
to just shut up, just empty every dumb
        dumb idiocy your own dumb mouth could slur.
Just so comparison can fail in that
        whose always more demands the more self same.
Or just as justice fails its wrongest needs
        just so the tab leaves out your every breath
which cannot write itself in any book
        but whose surmise exceeds elysium

The Unconditional

which I am not believed to mention now
        or any other pattern in the stars
since patterning is only from our selves
        and they resist all any every wish
huh
        uuuu! uuhuh-huh
Just as all these and many other things
        =x. had locked up and got into the car.
Before him in the immeasurable distance lay
        the ubiquitous tokens of false Agramant
his enemy whose signs were everywhere
        only not known as signage by the gulls.
Of what incomparable azure were
        the Kinneir placards which accosted him
at such velocities that even their
        once welfare modernist in clarity
essential messages disintegrate
        and let the important distances go by
and him so too get lost as best he could.
        The first stop was a real reality check.
The highway blacked out like comparison
        (bare were the feet that never tarmac knew
now first with delicatest steps inquiring
        how this ungrained exaction could

imprisoned in the concept none the less
        speak from beneath the bitumen or choke:
"For seventeen years I lay here. Seventeen
        more will be the round I not tread but make up
bruised by a violence ever disavowed.
        Not to have been born for me has been the worst
adventure drilled into my unresisting back.
        Just as for you die quickly is second best."
Around her scarce distinguishable songs
        of hornets, zodiacs, and of zephyrs were
immingled with the melancholy note
        which dark corsairs surrendered to the air
(a quieter growl than any other car;
        as quite unlike the fire spat by success
as also differing from gay Vauxhall;
        whilst imps and minxes demoniacally
shrilled from the all unthinking engines there:
        a jouissant chorus whose precise tone is
now irrecoverable as a passing strand
        of cirrus seen in 1963:
(whose not-fleece cloudishly resisting there
        reminds us that despite the morbid word
material specificity constitutively
        exceeds material specificity:

The Unconditional

making thought possible against the thought
        that every thought must nail itself to bed
inside a coffin of the historicized dead)
        (the more celestial machines become
the less they may be written in our books
        (as speaking goddesses devolve to dumb
reglazed deflectors of all godlike looks))
        or philosophic poem in the sand
eradicated by the evening tide
        (serving a better unconcealment thus
than any seen in its pedantic head
        as how much better in its death it thinks
than any saleable poet can alive:
        conclusively establishing in its
eroded blur the continuing life of thought)
        over defunct sierras now is heard
another note of triumphless disdain:
        the older threnody I scarce recall
(if threnody it may at all be called
        which only the corsair's lamenting voice
Fors seulement l'attente que je meure
        gave ought of less than martial to the ear:
then "demoniacally" might mean that
        the ineradicable blood washed off

could not in truth be thus washed off at all
        but rather took up daily residence
under a converted leisure centre outside Stevenage.
        Social Development Officials know
how not to sleep while silent Pylades
        beating the bounds of funding mutters one
violent instruction to put out the sun)
        thunderously shouted its maleficent wish
and shook the interior of each fiery car:
        another bass or velveteen cocoon
wraps fun-glum drivers of these later days))
        while maps inside the myriad carriages
intoned the toponyms with a feeling which
        owed much to the obliterated old
sheepwalks and military roads beneath
        (so each New sucks its death's blood from the last'
s sweetest cadaver which begins at once
        to putrefy and thus to smell of hope
as where there is nothing shit keeps heaven ope)
        and as much to the imminent burial still
of these brand newest highways under those
        whose traffic would by a power of many exceed
all power of road to hold them, bursting thus
        out to crack up the modestest little

The Unconditional

brick shopping terraces or rough hedgerows
        standing by. Where there is a map it is
always incredible verse should have died.
        It is the exacting outline of a realm
which makes concretion by abridgement or
        the hard and wiry line that always cuts
zygotically between the s and z
        donates to life life, thinking to the blood.
Block in town pink your unvisitable names
        map till we wish them to a zion grid.
Folk songs, meet a last end in the team coach.
        —""That always cuts?" ah but relationally"—
relationally I declare your szenery
        powerless to think a single word against
its own however disavowed true thought
        thunk in a soddenly resisting soul— —)
and =x. felt sorry for Tarmac but what to do.
        We must obey the Prince from A to Z.
As the cruel godnose when denied his food
        by any housewife in the neighbourhood
turns what they have to stone with pious glee
        creating epochs of resentment through
to revolutionists who from the church
        defenestrate the petrified cream cheese

The Unconditional

—a capital defeat for popery—
        and from unbleeding stump of all its stone
the superstitious foodstuff is well taught
        in future never to disturb the peace
learning the cream-cheese-eating vulgar there
        not to know better than to know this law
is all the church the future ever needs
        while their few amputate extremities
in miracles of distribution now
        are multiplied five thousand thousand fold
and stone across the waiting world is spread
        superior to perishable bread.
There was a lot of miles to drive and so
        into the green belt with a little twitch he
with subunfelt commiserating smile
        key-coughed to lurch off over the shoulder.
=x., nothing but the absence of himself,
        and taught to know this as his final lot
strove at each fragment of a second to
        avoid the amphiboly of believing him-
self real or other colourable stuff.
        The grandest feats of concentration there
strained to their own dispersal in the out-
        world worded as expectorated orts.

The Unconditional

Sad task to watch the tender concept die!
        Hard upon thinking to expel thinking
not once for all but over and again
        with an immense effort new at every least
infinitesimal or chance of life
        with difficulty thus to eject the ejecting power
and always lastly weeping violently
        over the failure of the void to void.
But in the hands of a master like =x.
        all this was happening on cruise control.
Bulk chunks of a complete cerulean slipped
        into the field of vision so prepared
blinking gelatinously treats in air
        and all was comfortably received by him
as the succession of facts about the world.
        He had to get to Harlow before dark.
In Hertfordshire the loneliest certainties are
        trod into pavements of the patient dust.
Pale brick watches them from a garden
        out-town without a town to be without
then multiplied times several to full
        a streetage never truly dark except
(and thus incapable of getting there
        at any certain time of day at all)

The Unconditional

in some miraculous power cut when
        a single insect sometimes may be heard
prophesying to the inhabitants our own existence.
        In Hertfordshire the mortal concepts do
live in some several instant of a flat
        choked apprehension of the rustling grass.
So sometimes when *September*'s reader does
        sense in the late September air a trace
or fears the absolute which after all
        is what a man-or-woman truly has
to fear in this life and not any thing
        which might come after it or not at all.
When there is menace in the cooling breeze
        or pleasing reminiscence of our death
hope for our unborn recollections flies
        taking the embodied form of an
effortlessly obsolete display of millinery.
        Park gates and old buses weep over the space.
Pushchairs comfort it under a cloth fringe.
        In that domain a buried A-road may
sometime by old pavilions of its shops
        remind a hoarse commercial traveller
of the remediable loss of life
        in undefended type face of a front

The Unconditional

still mutely pleading for the shoppers' loves
        still wearily enduring falling sales
still waiting for authenticated close
        or still abiding till a ripeness when
the properly intolerable come
        and foreclose closure closing it by force.
=x. was ready to feel all that.
        There or anywhere else.
But he was nowhere near the area.
        The hue of the metallic colouring on
his complicit vehicle accompanying him
        could barely properly be named as blue—
fantastically overpropertied
        as though blue left blue for a blue elsewhere
or settled only in the skull of an
        acatastatical erotomane
whose dream then taking vehicular form
        inflicts whatever violence it can
on any object-field whose lightest flinch
        might intimate a rustable flaw beneath
with a pure undersong of "blue, blue, blue".
        Serene irony fell into the wrong tax bracket.
Agramant flew six possible inches behind
        composing the thinkability of

The Unconditional

a radical evil or then radical good
        thinking the same conceivable in both.
The bus was not for everyone and so
        mage would prefer to ride whatever cloud
superfluously exits through exhaust
        or might have exited through any such
blocking true good and beautiful with all
        elaborate bare thinkability to kill
the here and now, irradiate with promise.
        In the fifth negation of aquamarine
determinately to recall that light
        or indeterminately colour it
making a shape of life at last grow old
        or not at last but in a single night
he laboured to efface all labour where
        his million minions painfully retrod
the air for him to speed his soaring path.
        Cobalts turned groaning from that blind potential;
ship or sky foundered into nothingness;
        sapphires just melted from their stylus and
of no more use then royally imploded.
        The imperial way of Agramante did
over these myriad negatings sing
        perfectly happiless in a top-rated kick

or how could it ever get better than this
        than this most murderous renouncing-feast
than this last outpost of a lost missed hue
        than this most cunning preservation of
this than this recollecting ever blue.
        Best bad infinity, your backlit smile
and shining flesh declare that inner will
        which lies in perfectible emptiness.
The more I strip the more I offer blood
        to every toxin loving to come in.
Propensity of poisons to invade
        the naked surface I propose to them
could reach this word, this breath, this bloodied est?
        I rip the surfaces from my inside
only to know the surfaces are there
        to know which is to know they are not me
(not so disowning but remembering all
        that could not only be inscribed in this):
My pronoun spews to offer no inside
        since none can show I have no side to me
(How is a sideless-suited suit-boy born?
        Can a boy-poison for his victim mourn?
"God ordered me to have some more to drink
        knowing without this I could hardly think")

The single strip which in a single kink
        portrays a sidedness against itself
triumphantly records without a mouth
        long after Euclid how there is no two
because a single slippage sings its one
        perfected twist of surfacelessness best
and snuffs you out with me and me with you
        or overcomes Cartesian dualists
in which meer outside if I utmost learn
        to gasp, choke, gag and know I hardly breathe
then "utmost" is the costly motto which
        reserves in its hyperbole a small
yet-yet existing remnant which in truth
        is just the absolute prohibited.
So say the Two in this inactual breath.
        =x. was looking for another part of the wood
but printers' were the only flowers there.
        Fat face rebawling from commission land
grimaced a price slab out and over me.
        Old face which I involuntarily bought
be you in 9-pt an antiquarian
        ie most abashedly not Baskervilleian
black voice of true inauthenticity.
        Shouted around or out thou cloth part of it

The Unconditional

I hope to vanish in an ever dusk
        or ever a dim glade light to show me
dark sobs translated to that greenery
        or paraphrased to eternal cypress there
resolve a one pink slip or fringed attire
        absolving error to oblivion there;
white blobs accomplished in that scenery
        recorded in a journal of no care
found from a silk or other wandering slip
        a like oblivion in her auburn hair;
Inviolably the virid summer gives
        its voluble warmth to every passing stare;
Obliviously the denuded body be
        embowered in loss from any hostile glare;
Inviolably the irradiate garment may
        give to inradiate flesh its wanted loss;
Obliviously the unshining soul may see
        the nonilluminable wood consume all gloss;
Inviolably then obliviate nor relive
        vile obviation till it never give
Obliviously then Inviola relieve
        the invidious violet of make believe.
Immortal mortals, mortal immortals
        [(or) mortal immortals, immortal mor-

The Unconditional

tals (or) immortals are mortal, mortals
        are immortal (or) immortals are mor-
tals, mortals are immortals, 'etc.'],
        living their death and dying their life.
Gravina goes under again to dwell (or).
        The salutary mages then retired
within delirio che sgombra
        and only thus preserved to after time
inefficacious knowledgeless their art.
        "I skulk in the pammiserible dust.
Forced to a crawl I cannot stomach a
        cold word of reason more than once a year.
I munch dirt as the only true food left
        much as you might eat corpses for the rest
and thus remove a poison from the world
        by load my every runnel bad inside."
"Then what you excrete must be credit?
        You must think Jobless that the old sun shines
out of the worse your diet still becomes.
        Savour it better would be really to taste
the dust in its each minute quiddity;
        your mastication flattens its outed abjects
until they qualialessly attest your name
        like an imaginary celestial choir

where nothing heavenly remains to hymn."
    "Thanks." Jobless went off out to check the post
ready to tear up the letter from Agramant
    which he was sure would any day arrive.
A thin house dust with traces of the dead
    lay quietly expiring on the sills
and other surfaces of his domain
    and calling to him with contralto voice
the dust asked pity which since still as yet
    it was impossible for him to give
to any thing so little absolute
    as mitochondria of the domestic world
ought more than shadowless perception he
    instead adjusted by an inch his jaw
adjusting thus the inadjustable loss
    inflicted on him daily by himself
or by whatever agency prevailed.
    Choirs of intolerable glory were indeed
his hourly companions in the aisles and malls
    where breaking him upon an endless wheel
they left his supper of retirement out.
    Choirs of intolerable glory did indeed
go with him in the streets and fields of death /
    Choirs of illimitably expanding need

The Unconditional

sang through his debits crediting with their breath /
   Choirs of necessitous limitation did
precisely scrutinize his impending fall /
   Choirs sadly lacking *désinvolture* would
constrictedly proscribe him after all.
   Immortal mortals, mortal immortal
(or)
  myself I suppose. Or else the whitest space
   will credit me with unsurpassable thoughts
I purchase without ever having to think.
   Cheap or twice.
Red patch, red patch.
   I break open now.
Crawl in and or live.
   It is T. going away in a car.
Please universal go to hell
   Data again shuttled
in curious pixels urgently to fill
   the alarming hiatus in consciousness,
then fell asleep.
   Narcotic consolations breathe a 0
from whose wrong absolute I cannot wake
   more than a colour is what just exists:
whether the grey retain its thousand shades

The Unconditional

        or whether in that greyness there be some
optative possibility of loss;
        whether the day remain vermilion or
remaindered probabilities emboss
        the poor sap with one lazy eye stuck on
the presence of this red patch here to consciousness
        or soul evacuated thus by the express
command of the protocol manager
        ("Oh yes alright then I can/cannot doubt
(tick one) the simple fact of sensing this
        this this, this this which you tell me again
is this red patch or objected example
        inducting me into the world of all
dry goods afloat in their negated world
        whose exemplarity is all they are
and where the concept only holds up for
        so long as the shrunk qualia verify.
A Red Patch instantaneously replied.
        "I this now here present myself to cs.
The thin red line which chokes down from my neck
        fixes me upright on the shining path.
Bisected frontage of a flaxen white
        falls off on either side from wrath
dropping in scarlet to ferocious wreck

The Unconditional

        of every morning after Attic night.
Through every tumult I keep going strong
        to my demise.
Know that I issue every warranting
        of warrantable living in the world.
Thus stuck mock or burlesquing it again
        you sell out to a heritage culture.
Superabounding saints already sang
        aeons before your effluating blurt
the whole true substance of your half defence.
        Every disavowed word you write is another
so-*man*nish screen off of the hard word.
        Primly turned wrongwards to an elder past
your stuffs stop clottedly it seems to me
        into an upper I earned innerwards
directed against its socalled innernesses
        or what is the problem really after all?
At last you must write your life just as it is."
        "Your certainty that what I write is mock
you may deliver to the mice and frogs.
        Since every fabulous precision must
to your ear drip and twist from nothingness
        into experience you file as blur
you can do nothing but reclassify

The Unconditional

    all real signifying as chimerical
and its words forcibly as insincere.
    The new as much escapes you as your death,
utterly unable to receive its ash
    into your progress-avid ajar jaw
hung dumbly open to receive the worst
    whatever other dropped into it and
smacking your lips then to forget the taste
    misnaming destiny whatever dirt
you first oblige yourself to eat then sing.
    First self-applaud in nylon then in rags.
You modernize your skin for tags.
    Avidly irreversibility
you gulp down hurling headfirst off a rock
    taking for oxygen general despair
each vain pique prinked up in your head can draw
    breath of not-nothing from its not-the-worst
semi-asphyxiation till the grave
    or other kind oblivion come to save.
I write what gets taken into my mouth.
    Just as it is I can and do affirm,
just as it undelimitably is,
    just as a single affirmation sings
the tunelessest selected tesseral

              or Age of Prose like no prose ever heard
age not of prose but rather of a dim
              laborious deafness as the condition of—
just as it is or just as it is not—
              as at some point I false first person must
gutter to drop the outsided double me
              so this parenthesis will never close.
Just as it is and only then unlocked
              when from a scrap of printed music drops
some paper memory or prompting mote
              unsealing tarmacked-over singulars
anagramatically from the heart
              alone to rescue life from dying art
nu hony in a B saves from starvation next.
              Where is the bloody example? Where but on
the bloody cross? Whose concept covers it?
              Whose but his own or eating innerwards
incarnately to devour the difference
              present the sickening self-punishment
brisk M. Dionysus will class insane
              who sections this 'unable to have fun:
'refusing thus the only one command
              'given to mortals on this little earth:
'withhold stipend until further notice.'"

The Patch drew itself up to its full height.
"Your mouth gets taken with a count by rote?
        You seriously expect us to believe
what you thus whimper of your ancestors?
        I know for a fact that some of them were
no better than they ought to have been at all.
        Your catachreses call for some remark.
I "gulp" "despair" I take for "oxygen"?
        "Precisions" "drip" or "twist"? I "file as blur"?
Already the poor letter of the truth
        is quite concealed by hazy metaphor
from which you too precociously concoct
        the mingled element which permits and hides
the ailing fantasies you would sell on
        as voice-of-History or just of-God.
Blackmore's *Creation* rewritten by
        a third-class imitator of Beau Brummell!
Henry More of our era except no good
        please sing your song of the soul into the sink.
Swinburne would have despised you."
        A show of fist fight followed, and then calm.
It was after all true that the mouth had more
        to do than merely write, and even true
that mouths could never write except in some

The Unconditional

        perverse recombination of events;
the milky depression in a plastic cup
        in this sense mouths to the recipient mouth
its panillitigable message of
        x 'caution contents hot' a word which now
admits its untruth on a pavement tar.
        This muttered treatise then was self-addressed.
"What he called borrowed feathers are my skin;
        are rather the immediate inside of that
art deeply hidden in the human soul
        which makes all possible science possible,
yet which extends its real kingdom far
        beyond that meanly transcendental task—
since transcendental rules the inside out
        and also rules the outside out as well
leaving for measure a poor equals x
        or happiest remnant known to live in hell—
the experience which it really enables does
        in struckthrough plush or decommissioned steel
explode from the interior the blind list
        of categories into a hundred possible thoughts.
So to the sick twelve merely handed down
        succeed a myriad fundamental names.
Traditionlessness munches its own stump

The Unconditional

        or turns to nothing all it squats upon.
Tradition turning out tradition into
        the immiserated world unspell us quite.
Steeped in those colours over and again
        at last the dye takes in your fingerprint
colouring all tests with one needful hue
        perfectly single out into the air."
Into that world when we do try to walk
        we walk into no out that is not here
already in the outworlded homeless house
        ex-extrajecting personned worlds
as the forlornest armchair on the earth
        intones in contrabass its sole career
embodying the inobligable paradise
        which frees us from relation with a sale.
Corpse-dinner Homebase dizzyingly ascend
        from off this land into a higher air
in which to place your church dogmatics of
        an incontaminable freedom we
with every vengeful purchase that we make
        assert by killing maiming suffocating since
fatal indifference brings us off the best
        when sexual absolutes put us to the test.
Lunch off the gap to fervent ecstasy.

The Unconditional

       Then eat more daily to prevent the nadir
shading the edge of the virtual mirror.
       If you go far enough to turn the skin back
the plasms will invert their proper place
       leaving you gazing with a crazy stare
over the coldest and the meanest life
       with no more meaning than just swallowing
your own saliva like you do anyway.
       You is they but it dunt know that.
The fundamental names rolled up for more.
       Or will you swear to Arbitrariness
those saints whose names you bear were false?
       Their most astonishing swerves the more
attest a straight track into kingdom come.
       The vehicle had hit a hilly patch.
The proper smoothness of the public road
       rising and dipping to reveal or hide
a lit extent of lightly shimmering grey
       grey-blue and grey-green hazily dispersed
with some grey-silver rarely interspersed
       where metal fixtures caught the greyish light
foregroundlessly at once surprising sight
       with indiscriminable shades of light
or indiscriminable at any speed

The Unconditional

> sustainable on the highway motoring down
beneath soft kisses of his smoothing wheels
> > prostrating themselves over and again
against the inexorably patient stuff.
> > > The car felt fit to lift up from its bed
of downy asphalt packed beneath its path
> > > > so that for an instant =x. felt his own head
lift for a second from its securing neck
> > > > > not unallied to madness in the bone
and take flight into the lip of a curve
> > > > > > off out over the bright land but in the
air with brightness glimmering from its stump
> > > > > > > provoking (since his head in fact
remained stuck to its lumpen body there)
> > > > > > > > this reminiscence of a holiday
where every day his car had seemed to fly
> > > > > > > > > into narrated mountainscapes of pink-
grey or pink, pink-grey, pink and grey or blue
> > > > > > > > > > yet where the coloration was a 0
to the presented prospect when the car
> > > > > > > > > > > slipped down a hill and looked up to the north
to see a single line of mountains sing
> > > > > > > > > > > > across the available field of vision there
entirely like a single line of verse

The Unconditional

        caught by an accident in middle air
and stating its complete extent at once
        with perfect snowy candour to the view
and demonstrating in its contour that
        there is no writing that may not be cut
by mountainously determinate outlines which
        best understand their own poetical
relation to the legion catalogues
        of actual lights which cannot actually
recur at any time with any same
        light but always differ as the daemmering
dumb golden gloriously scarifies
        so called grand or at least visible light
or shade in each refusing serif there.
        An underthought of danger mixed itself
with briefest reminiscence in this thought
        which occupied a fragment of a tick
of the loud clock in every person's brain
        —momentum written on no front of song
like motion trying to accelerate
        until it reaches that peculiar speed
at which a quantity to quality
        retransubstantiates unnoticedly
and dance as if no member were not drunk

        or rather scattered into life than sunk
as though want's dummy powering engines there
        could break its circuit into painful life
from motion moving movelessly inside
        contexts of immanence it treads around
to break by force of desperation out into
        not-nothing's metalogical outside
or phantasmatically as though we shone
        fairest in trains of spectral emptiness
just as the pianoforte repertoire
        falls speechless in the 1820s when
it passionately blots out every pause
        in essenceless becoming circling
as keyboard campanologists of steam
        would unlock clockwork with its own docked cog
feeling the felt clicked by the hammered wood
        with torqued mimesis of an insect there
or as a Montesquiou by turns will plead
        or turn by rage cum wheedle to seduce
inflict developments upon one phrase
        it rounds upon and back to ceaselessly
awaiting progress in recorded sound
        for the device of fade out it demands
incompetent to end or to begin

The Unconditional

        and in this truly inessential glut
bawling to mummy with a tour de force
        best cantus firmus of essential shells
most inexpressive in their tenderness
        still most rapacious where they most co-weep
still kindest in the dissonance they keep
        when pressed with violence to the bleeding ear
drowning the oceans in their engine roar
        and bearing with them all that listeners risk
until they clatter with a loud report
        into the effigy of final shock
hoping by sheer noise to resuscitate
        the torpid letter hearts out in the hall.
Anything else just sounds stupid.
        Commas and points I rub out from the white
wishing to set by absence all to right.
        A locomotive melancholy drones
in cumulative grace notes from the page.
        I knew myself condemned to re-enact
chapter to chapter in my freest acts
        all the wrong footnotes to Augustine which
—one who by veneration well forgot
        was most unheard where most reprinted then—
had specified the facia on the desk

The Unconditional

        where all my credit notes were written and
had specified the facial detail where
        I most expressed my innermost true self
now Baianist now Jansenist nor true
        and there most false where most at letter stuck
of spirit-shelteringly petrified re-trucked
        like Bayerische Motors when they stream
out of North London every last weekend
        heading with black inexorable snout
to heart treats wafted from the golden east
        often as far afield as Deptford nose
abashed to find their selves in, what,
        the last best listed public housing found
this side of Keats and Shelley Terraces
        (if any kindness or if tenderness
still at some fingertip of cognitive
        ensouled ensouling touch still may remain
they are my teeth and claws of human war
        a thought which has me almost fit to weep
the perfect razor from my animal
        and rational and thus my cruel eyes
before indifference ever sleepily
        come to recover me into its blue
beyond of parallel impossible

The Unconditional

        normal barbiturate neutrality:
How may I motorisch Metromanie
        retune the obsolete engine of a You
so it may sing with no less silken growl
        sounding expensive nor obtained for free
off of the bits of rubbish on the street
        sliding with inverse wish to the sedan
rusting without resentment every claw?
        Union of Washerwomen Poets reascend
shedding all cruel personae from your flight!
        Gobsmack the ironists with one well judged clout
diving to soar across all register
        taking a single sheer delicious curve
judged to that tensile and to that relaxed
        exactly placed decisive serpentine
which as there is one only frequency
        in any given set of givens which
will shatter on condition that it is
        made with that art that makes it real glass
will violencelessly with a sung caress
        bring to a million pieces High or Low
or float a measure out of up or down
        both in your dances and in those of life!
Bob now red dolphins and then just exclaim

The Unconditional

        with the popped tiptop marks to their pink
elation everywhere beside itself!)
        so with less capital I ran to sump
unknown to hear in a cloth ear of print
        more of methectic numeration than
the scrambled cipher heading up a blob
        of electronic routage from the gob
e-glossolalially spoke off knob.
        "That question is poorly formed."
Stuffed angels on a dummy pinhead marked
        Victims of Useless Speculation and
made from spoilt ballots of the sunshine state
        shredded together with the libraries of
some bankrupt schools of old divinity
        remasticated thousandthousandfold
and slipped with delicacy from the mouth
        by highly professional termites labouring
at dioramic fixture set up by
        the labours of a hundred editors
mutely shout out to the complaining souls
        "We exemplify over-precise questioning!
In the end just shut up and accept the result!
        Know you, persisting, papery ends will meet.
That sharp you'll cut yourself or else we will."

The Unconditional

        Euhemeristically macerate
into celebrities the falling gods.
        May hero medals of usefulness instead gleam
from every funded filling of your mouth.
        May your suit never thin to any sheen
wrapping its woolly function up in drouth.
        When we say one we not say one-of-all.
We not say one and not the other nor
        do we say one not many or at all
oppose the one to anything at all.
        We drive the spirit to that perfect pitch
at which an absolute contingency
        is only able to stand in for it.
A thought's best picture of it shelters in
        the aspirate on ɛ in the word 'ɛv.
Pointing at last is all the speech I know
        without which tense and urgent matter slides
off from the conversation into air.
        I disquotationally preadjust
all losses into whiteness with a swipe
        of cursive energies I first command
within a menu at no table where
        I must say I eat very well for now.
I eat very well for now.—

The Unconditional

        bringing to =x. the tiniest perception that
(just at the instant when was chanted out
        in recollection by the floating chain
of aerial Oquirrhs what they knew of all
        the invincibility of human sin
and with it thus the indefeasible
        co-worst Idea of good by every peak
declared and uttered in redundant stone
        where without Y in legible alphabet
volcanic foliage its furthest leaf
        caused in a movement of the lower arm
to shift the wheel in sympathy with this
        (Richest petroleum notes or choc crowded
the rear throat and nose with their gloom Rothko
        could hardly more a psychopomp have keened
with darkished pan-purpurealistic moos
        or other lowings in the holy place:
=x. opened his trap wide to get the full
        effect of it reflecting all the while
on how by error may sometimes be saved
        a vanishingly arch-archaic glimpse
(a truth he once remembered hearing best
        delivered in a lecture on Cortot
whose text and title then diverted him

    attempting as he drove to reconstruct.
"The wrong note: A. Cortot as medium.
    A photograph of the pianist on my wall
shows him conducting an orchestral piece.
    All the surroundings have been lost in gloom.
From a murky pool of light in the middle
    of the picture C. himself looms up.
His left arm is drawn hard across his chest
    thrusting a tiny white stick to the right.
The torso topples forward to the gaze
    as though the conductor is in danger
actually of falling over from the force
    of meant intensity felt by this stroke.
The eyes are hollow caves of sorrow which
    appear to moan an imprecation out.
The whole is dressed in an ill fitting suit.
    Precisely in his getup Cortot well knew
just how to strike the very wrong note
    so prestidigitatorily false
yet none the less re-echoing to us
    a music barely legible today.
Something of the wish embodied in
    that music-making pose the picture saw
must stick forever to whatever art

        however disenchantedly pursues
its still-persisting minutely detailed
        truth in the slightest twitch of force or tone.
He makes up only what's already there.
        The comical yet also serious pathos here
finds possibly a pianistic match
        in a small passage from an early record
made of C. playing Schumann: the final
        long variation from the symphonic
studies, bar 15 (here without repeat)
        in 1929 in Small Queen's Hall.
Only the sketchiest attempt at all
        seems to be made at rendering the notes.
That passage of the record is as though
        the pianist should not play but invoke
the score before our eyes – "you know the rest".
        Those wrong notes none the less reverse disdain
or generous negligence of the minute
        —as when a man would rather choke to death
than ever ask for water to wash down
        the roasted salmon backs and so avoids
the at once magnanimous and fatal meal
        or would himself roast in his rival's fire
which hospitably burns his relatives

The Unconditional

        all who must royally enjoy themselves
and comment on the pleasurable heat:
        a universe of death in Brummell's tie
whose line cuts out the heart of every weak
        poor imitative proto-dandy when—
"Meyers Lexicon had reached the letter S.
        At last I could learn about sonata form"—
its absolute perfection first is seen:
        the aptest prophet of whose worldly lack
long since had died in Africa, not before
        delivering forgotten sermons there
which none the less more closely understand
        their least tie-pin than any other hand:
"CHANGE not always IMPROVEMENT.
        This hostelry of ours if versiform
then oriental depilation strips
        as the discission of a total swoop
invests the sea with a quite novel vice
        now not of vomiting but eating wrecks
or then all smoothliest in living death
        effeminated even as to his ear
had he not heard the clarion call
        and had persisted in his maidenhood
(in infinitesimal pulse of this recall

The Unconditional

        which opened out into a moony space
=x. quailed with ecstasy and terror there
        tempted to lose his life and save it there
tempted to cross the line erasing there
        all memory of irrecoverable loss
tempted just to collapse nor saving there
        ought hope of ought more than remaining loss
tempted to cave in instantaneous joy
        floated on centuries of eating dross
(and at the idea of this temptation he
        westering at once into the freezing rain
foresaw renouncers in the frozen waste
        hallucinating infinite delight
as less by less still gave that joy increase
        and at that instant he at once foreheard
the most archaic and the newest voice
        singing a logic in resistless air
only to be made intelligible by
        responsive burst of effort from his lung
emphatical in melodies of tense
        antiphonal felt impulse in the throat
—for listening is mutest speaking where
        the air we gulp in gulps out from the breast
just as the light bird cuts an airy way

The Unconditional

         the better for reality of air
borne up by what resists it better than
         an unresisting nothing ever can—
and no more refutable than the wind
         nor more translatable than mountainsides
yet left the blackened remnant of its stuffs
         translated into coptic by the nuns
whose widely now derided loving care
         delivered this small pamphlet by balloon:
ONly immiserible life can tell
         why copia copies out at all a truth:
ONly the precrescendal mind in hell
         knows why the copyist copies any truth:
an old mutation of the modern mind
         gives to the singular every poorest best:
a new-old reinvention of the kind
         returns to copiousness its lack of test:
as frozen wastes are warmer in the zone
         where heating makes them partially at home
so when a falsest rigour comes to rest
         its worser impulses begin to home.
From colons semicolons multiply.
         Logic at length in lists must surely die.
Then twice as long as Milton trot along

The Unconditional

        to prove to Daddy-o the worthless song
while all deforestations gathering
        murmur the blankness of the thoughts you sing
with pen and ink or worse recorded still
        in the bad binaries of e-Quecoatzil.
This IS the broken lighted triple word
        lighting whose daylight audible as sound
redoubles irredundantly its force
        donating not a penny to the thing
and not a penny either to the thought
        where wordlessly evacuated space
retransubstantiates its nothings there
        with galimatias from u to s
and back again from s to u at once
        so instantaneously and not at all
gliding end gliding back from 0 to 0
        wishing to empty rather than to fill
yet if I sooner utter let there be
        optatively by repetition I
break open from its smooth erasure there
        a dry skin on my skin and killing it
break my bone open to the speaking wind
        becoming utterly incapable
of not receiving broken life as life

The Unconditional

        nor broken open less in love than grief
shedding the stupid skin of unbelief
        or breaking no more broken than the wave
dash on the shore whatever ocean gave
        returning ceaselessly to recommence
still unremaking and rebreaking thence
        still in a scale of music cut with skill
all sounding future alphabets of will
        still in a painted breath to mark the sound
illimitably replicate unbound
        still from its still exhaustible return
still as exhaustibly the sun can burn
        as unindifferently beats the sea
on rocks on sand on darkness and on me
        and with a language no less written there
left on the skin of all this salt in air
        O, hear
hear this
        voc-vocative imperative performed
recalling empty noise without a name
        hear this cry falling vainly to the shore
hear song which would untune itself and die
        incapable of stammering the one name
light that will ever darken nevermore

The Unconditional

        hear in inaudible blue the ocean roar
or make this heart break or beat out again
        the single rhythm life returns to pain
no help for it but cutting ever comes
        help for it cuts form coming overcomes
strike hard strike once then never once again
        struck through then struck down striking for the main
lie down upon the grass and weep once more
        once more to shatter fallen leaves the poor
then scatter limbs through each of which is wrote
        music that proves the learning self by rote))
had otherwise been married to some man—
        behold accordingly mutation here
in double monstering from man to girl
        and girl to man at once remonstering back:
more doubly monstrous for confessing this
        than for the first deception first deceived:
yet far less monstrous than when monstrous lust
        performed the non-maternal version through:
the club preferred to reek with beaten brains!
        Pestered with unguents as it hourly was!
What sort of person he was in that silk
        can only inferentially be known
by thinking what she was in lionskins

The Unconditional

        deodorizing them painstakingly
—a process which I venture here to hope
        was there effected by balsamic salve
always supposing that the mane too there
        submitted to the well-bejewelled comb—
the yawning mouth closed up with other hair!
        The jaw-teeth overshadowed by the fringe!
The whole outraged visage would have roared
        had it been able to and not been stuffed.
I know what you are going to say to this.
        "Empedocles wore silk and brazen sandals too."
Yes, and much good his cymbal-footwear did him!
        If at that moment from his barking tub
Diogenes had leapt with muddy feet
        he had not merely muddied all that vest
but carried wholesale to the sewer-nymphs
        or under-slaughterhouse of popular lusts
that man who thought himself celestial
        that he might as a god salute the dung
and afterwards bring news of it to earth:
        "What sort of a coat is that maniac wearing?"—
leaves marine conchs and tritons sojourning
        eager to prove to Plato that the heights
decursively dismutating decay—

    and would that Asia were by this time too
no longer fearful of the hungry soil
    and would that Africa had once for all
before the devouring chasm lastly quailed—
    whilst other fashionable detriments
make martial innovations on the earth
    eyes utterly Homeric or eyes closed
may see that day and night revolve in turn;
    a tardigrade field-hunting quadriped—
the tortoise of Pacuvius, you think?
    There is another beastling which it fits—
get on all fours and try it out yourself—
    who airs her swelling silk, consoles her neck
more impure than her sty with necklaces
    & fits on impure leg pink shoe or white
so corpse-bearer and pimp and lecturer
    rivalling Physco in perversity
all walk together in the fatal hour.
    Who may exsuppurate these purulencies?
Yes, of a Fifth I also know the tale.
    Whose bruises stink from wickedness can say
how many work-hours washed the bedsheet clean
    or who bent down to pick the bloody crumbs
off of a dog out in the garden shed.

"All that is liberal in studies lies
under my four old angles. My mere sight
          beats eyes of vices downward to the dust.
Tongueless philosophy in my speaking cut
          sings down the idle chatter of the schools."
Well, so speaks plain old Mantle! Leave me now
          as calmly as you can; and may happiness
once and for all resistibly dissolve
          over the surface of your resting mind."
In which imperial republic we
          skulk as the obligated subjects of
equalitarian moguls as they lounge
          from suit to suit hung by the neck till dead—
rather in just those errors the discredited
          Idea may shelter for a little space
in slips and clusters of a truthful luck
          until its annihilation at the hands
of a well-armed and militant regiment
          of teenage virtuosi dexterously destroyed."
(Several such at this point exited.
          "Still wouldn't Cortot have been better if
he hadn't played so many wrong notes?" "No."
          Several more departed.) The lecturer
warmed to his task of driving every one

                    of these professionals to leave the room.
"The Idea, as I was saying…" Only five
          were left now: =x., C. himself of course, T.,
young Wiesengrund and someone else
          whom nobody remembered having met.
"The Idea we make the reflex target of
          our own wish not to believe it possible—
a wish which by no means has any good
          in it but rather the reverse desire
to put ourselves for ever in the right
          however cruelly or lumpish we
might act or think—which cruelty itself
          we raise in fact to a denied Idea
forever struck through but forever king
          of the ressentimental realm's despair—
this though the scope is small for any one
          performer most of all ever to sing,
bound down as all interpretation must
          be to whatever object it attends—
almost no glimpse of it can ever look
          through inauthentic authenticity
or superinhuman effort misrespent
          chained to the fatal letter of the law—
chained to its second family of hate—

The Unconditional

        it is of *this* Idea that the absence of
the right notes in that Schumann passage speaks—
        speaks with mute music of negation here
which I invite you now to listen to."
        A bulky machine was wheeled out to the front.
T. was asleep, C. dead, and Wiesengrund
        was making furious notes for a riposte
which doubtless would consume the evening too.
        =x. tried to remember the other one.
He must have been someone significant.
        A pallid possible smile, a bluish skin—
indefinite grandeur of a malign thin
        countenance which played around the eyes—
as with a dawning terror =x. felt his mind slip)
        renewed determination of the real
as really making up the real true
        and ineliminably meaningful)
he might be about to have an accident
        before which the approaching truck already swerved
and left long afterechoes of its horn
        (the lone or saddest sound I ever heard
loosed from a crane or goose and amplified
        through longer seconds in the shuddering air)
while he sat up quick at a jolt in panic

> Do you not remember that you admitted that the art of reciting verses was different from that of driving chariots?

The Unconditional

        (something had nearly happened and so he
was nearly happy, driving on with a new
        stamped cheerful countenance into what would
come around the next corner to greet him)
        and then sat up twice when he saw the blood
come really bubbling down his helpless chin
        while in his inner ear a pure noise
was by long labour painfully reworked
        till it rejoined the thought of crumpling steel
in this sub-second of 183 lines
        which was the time in which he then blacked out.
With his own broken bones he doubted there
        that fear of error was really the error itself.
Bright as the little scarlet trickling from
        his face he once for all undoubted there—
(just as just now en abandon de geste
        with all the lassitude bad weather brings
disesperating every afternoon
        I tell the rosary of library hours
I love to follow lights amid the storm
        where undergoes exquisite crisis here
verse-eaten but above ground I decline
        or shudder at disturbance of the veil
or little tears appearing in those folds

The Unconditional

        as verse was only waiting for his death
then to collapse itself with all relief
        yet shelter in a finer tact or box
until the time to jump up from the muck
        exposing sword or flower to the view
to decorate or kill according as
        the metrical agalma there may serve
occasion of delight or punishment
        bestowing efficaciously accords
of neighbouring tonalities upon
        the hidden absolute he still conceals
until still bashful coming to an end
        all proud and naked he at once displays
imperishable alexandrines there
        where the eleventh and the thirteenth fail
as sharply different from a holiday
        taken too loosely from exhausted moulds
initiating into certain charms
        eternally seductively the false
as equally from the numerating clerks
        patiently calculating up to twelve
then no less rarely than the national flag
        is national cadence properly employed
as reminiscence of the strictest line

The Unconditional

        spectrally stalks such centrifugal games
conferring on them spectral surplus where
        every one has her proper pipe or viol
to sound for each peculiar one soul
        the proper melody and proper death
as disappointingly as night remains
        the brightest word communicated down
so disappointingly when day contains
        the darkest shadows language ever frowned
or write without accessories at dusk
        as verseless thinking crumbles into dust
and is the subject of next 21 lines
        finding instead of glory only this
old prohibition on the absolute
        which since there never can be any first
or total language there before condemns
        all spastic tongues to babble in a bib
brave as an infant hearing language now
        or luminated as a thinking face
then by its clinging to that single suck
        most miserably contracted of brow
in desperate refusal of a fuck
        nestling the best in any freezing place
so stuck or emulous of infant joy

          as to insist its pleasures must be fear
or hatred written in its mother's face
          while only to protect the critic cry
wawling remembrance of a solar boy
          it gives its own best hope a muffled thump
warm in skip huddle like a blessed lump
          nor never find within itself the power
materially in a single strike
          to utter coin metallically true
in which case verse would instantly decay
          or rather shrivel to dimensionless
prenihilated nothing worsting there
          the strange arcanum voiced in elder time
and in its long decay affording soil
          for unheard plants mocking the poet's toil
as ideas that this liberation lets
          each poet string out from Her reedy breath
her solely singular and propertied
          substantial prosody from her own breath
"—to say nothing of his own spelling system!—
          The joke laughs loud aloud or then inspires
the platform of preface writers [whatever
          that is] and is simply ridiculous.
That kind of thing is fodder for the newspaper boys."

The Unconditional

        Shut up in infinite translation then
revomiting from this revomited
        incompetently englished afterbirth
the mere reporting which ubiquitous
        ly babbles over the whole field
brute or immediate here but there designed
        by essence and essential lineaments
or silently to place in a strange hand
        the silent tessera silently to say
truth in the body silently decays.
        Then international free verse taking flight
bound without limit to the yielding air
        in immemorial possibility
of falling otherwise than in repair
        melting a crust of habit from the eye
and thus permitting me at last to hear
        all visible escaping from that spell
things in themselves which well can move about
        on road or field and in the gentle rain
at last into their own reality
        as when a front door opening with a click
allows some single breath of air into
        a warm house insulated from the wind
which falls upon the drying cheek to tell

        of all unspeakable contingency
and thus alone by temperature sings
        an *Öffnet dich* in colours of the sun
or clarion shedding irony to lose
        all sound of other than the Real itself
which to this poem is forever locked
        unless by accident some new surprise
shall break me open into new demise)
        —that there is lived experience on this earth.
Long then the interior pathways which were trod
        by whatever did the treading in that black.
Above he lay chained to his sublunar bed.
        Below that hospital worked a storying power
a hundredfold in subjectless narratives—
        =x. or =x.- on a traffic isle
could in the advancing gale of carbon not
        get his one foot or mouth to take a step
further than would be blown back by the wind
        of oleaginous byproducts flung
from the most terrible grilles and drums he saw
        power on towards him with invincible haste.
Wishing to cross but rooted to the spot
        an older power anchored him to earth
and to its still unvanquished deities

    as Raven Mask Car yawned into his face
exposing the ferocious chrome inside
    Wrong Round The World began to eat his shoes
demanding blankets tearfully with stabs
    so that the only possible escape
was a dreamt alibi releasing him
    from all this pain by first informing him
that all this pain was only dreamt and so
    it was time to repeat the giantkilling dream
and from that exit to the deepest sleep
    or dream of morphine in 'a council flat'.
Wet paper flapped at his rubbery face;
    a cold little wind got under the coat;
these were the details of a latest dream
    of waking up which often re-appeared
just when the god supply had been switched off
    (back to East Carbon without engine brakes
or down to Chromo colourblindly fly)
    and only when the morphine came back in
could he again resume his favourite thoughts
    (thought in a dream but no less thought for that
as think both wakingly and when asleep
    is what in all however thoughtless hours
my thoughtless-thinking soul must ever do.

† Diamond. *I thirst for useful drink.*
† Incinerated moth. *My Life In Glamour.*
　　† The lamp and idol. *Insert coin here for light.*
† Narcissus. *Die enough first or twice.*
　　† The sun and candle.
† The spinners. *Deteriorating surface.*
　　† Target. *Die of prolonged recalcitrance.*
† Phoenix. *Bomber life.*
　　† The bird in lime. *My name is Metaphor.*
† Dido in flames. *Woodcut oblivion.*
　　† Weathervane. *Moveless of twisters winded.*
† Heliotrope. *The flight of capital.*
　　† The wall and ivy. *I love by smothering.*
† Deer.
　　† Actaeon. *Fail to be torn apart.*
† Orpheus. *Poet in racing blinkers.*
　　† The basilisk and mirror. *No free lunch.*
† Two broken oars.
　　† False coin. *I sink all possible errors.*
† Alembic.
　　† Unicorn sees itself. *No motto.*
† The viper suicide. *In human animal.*
　　† Armourer. *Polished by friendly fire.*
† Saw. *Proverbs cut twice or sharper first.*

† Two queens with snakes.
† The muleteer. *A 14.*
　　† The cat and rattrap. *Theme or close down.*
† Peacock.
　　† The moon in darkness. *Their* esse *is* percipi.
† The twice-dulled coin)
　　　　reminding him of how he used to dream
of Hertfordshire's innumerable roads
　　　　in numberable sequence of a grey
　　　　and cool green summer where the assembled clouds
spoke slightest shifts of light or dark grey out
　　　　or where minutely to the luxurious verge
the pavement sang a different shade of grey
　　　　bespeaking in its asphalt icing there
too blissful intimations of a care
　　　　taken by someone he would never know
ensuring safety on the roads or so
　　　　and thus enfolding in the public's love
all private flight to fantasized above
　　　　so turning greywards then each careful thought
where active frontages a feature make
　　　　to sequence volumes through the signage there
as visual rhythms nothing it to top
　　　　the topcapped lighting scoping the return

The Unconditional

complete a language never really so
        of stone or metal by that token thus
losing their surfaces to sheer caprice
        where all their silk or gravel blanks again
too well deleted by the user name.
        Once more the grandest stops of tedium
open suave choruses of civic song
        while some unhelpful wreckers at the back
raise points of order as they age and die
        to the subdued professionals who wring
all pathos of administration out
        of our least grimace or grey handkerchief
how bravely bearing out the iron cage
        burnt on the eye and burnt into the ear
while bearing still the counterburden too
        of human being cold to just be kind.
The difficult burn up in agonies.
        The helpful soothe them with a pack of lies.
How calm and gentle we proceeded still
        while charming exquisites ascended by
bidding their dibble dribble gob a glib
        big dose of flatus vocis in the head.
=x. slept still walking in six thousand years.
        The report had to be ready for the chair.

Chair for report was readied too by much.
        Report was progressed to another group.
Group then would scope it for a group or such.
        Keen we are liturgies we eagerly
Keen we are keen are keen of course to see
        much eager progress in the liturgy
"Wer sagt Kultur sagt auch Verwaltung mate:
        if you don't like it why not prove it please
by living in a 2 by 2-4 box
        marked Soviet Sentiments of Comrade Jarvis,
eh?" Then fist in stomach can refute it thus.
        Grief is a species of idleness.
With what harsh effort must I wander then
        so by refinement polished scarred and lopt
till every comfortable rust removed
        I shine with vacancy from every cell
and everyone who sees me in the street
        can see his face in me before he cuts
away to other mirrors otherwhere
        wishing to ramble back to childish joys
whose signature lies in the now erased
        and well obliviated summa still.
Idleness is a kind of grief.
        Pray without ceasing hums from every dim

unsleeping traffic signal on the block.
        I fruitless roam from shop to rosy shop
and almost gagging at the herbal sweets
        I scarce to the most temperate breath alive
handling my own limbs like a stick of rock
        hoping to make that only purchase which
may be a type of labour by its one
        irreplicable singularity:
driven from shelf to shelf by fancyings
        to find that object which does not exist
and thus to spend with irreproachable
        propriety the extra from some sump
as Ariostos of modernity
        tumbling upon a blunt impossibility
made by ejection of my own alive
        "Indolence is the grief of species, not
out-knowing but -bearing its core-cum-surface
        reflective component".
Jobless went out to get the shopping in.
        =x. woke up with a bone in the throat (or).
Agramant hovered not-outside the text.
        Jobless took rubbish outside to the bin
while =x. bewept incessantly his fears
        thinking that Agramant would be the next

The Unconditional

blow to hit Jobless rupturing the skin
        inverting =x. so that a wound appears
immedicably festering in hexed
        or Agrammantic poisons working in
while Jobless' daughters scorning him to tears
        unpick the thin web holding up '=x.
exposing his self flattery as sin
        and phoning Agramant who at once steers
his car at Jobless walking out for sex
        which caves =x. inwards from his outside in.
Agramant rubbed his sticky eyelids clean.
        Or rubbed half-open from their sealing glue.
He was not going to pay Jobless for what
        Jobless would do in any case for free.
He was not going to write to Jobless.
        Deduce my pen.
The rain blobbed window glinted indigo
        and sundry other shadings through a blear
white water held its taut menisci up
        in several drops across the dirty glass
as though an archipelago of goods
        were separately islanded for sale
in patterns which no real sales logic had
        dispersed across a filthy thickened glaze

The Unconditional

presenting through its smeary filter there
        the memory or hope of an outside
taking the shape of grey or pastel cars
        lumbering indistinctly through the rain
nor ever using any power to hurt
        but pausing at the crossings of the road
and floating in this way the everyday
        fine medium of ordinary life
with barely perceptible menace thinned
        which drifted inside as the slightest thought
refracted through the waxy water drops
        turning in passages the square cars round
in scattered spheres of off white or scratched chrome
        stuck on the glass distortingly unseen
continuous unease which settled in
        to Agramant's too variable heart
as the erratic rhythm of collapse
        brought to reflection by a blip of blood
sounding irregular in his left ear
        and causing him almost to miss just what
he had been sitting there for all day long
        as only when the more than blue GrandAm
had disappeared five seconds since did he
        leap up at a gap and grab his coat and keys

while the blood hammered in his ailing head
        (as when an eye beam first re-doubted light
a consort soul could never credit this
        if not by brilliantly confecting there
still more adventures of its own devising
        still in this pit advancing and retreating
still of its expiration making rising
        still at this end methodically bleating:
so worst is still converted to the best
        by every exhalation of its dying
as any other wastage meets the test
        or secret standard of the loudest crying))
or tamely then decide to do your worst
        since where the worst is then the slip of good
must surely nestle on its obverse face
        known by complete negation of its truth
forming itself in Agrammantic plans
        or plans of imitators who would find a port
("since perfect hatred still does in its kind
        have something perfect let us total it":
castrate Manhattan in a double smash
        (yet what ensues is miserable light
wretchedly dawning on a scene still there
        and rather through a residue of brick

The Unconditional

whistling a stupid ditty to the sky
        than panabolishedly caving in
in perfect recollection of the act
        (yet what ensues is this and this and this
particular wreckage of ten thousand skins
        which now no longer work or shelter there
living and breathing their once grateful souls
        or yet if I might lend their wounds a voice
seem not to mourn nor not not to rejoice
        nor have they anything of glass to shine
the silvered perfects back to self in time
        (then what ensues is breath and milk and bread
pouring their goodness on the hating dead:
        just as I choose the hardest efficacious word
to hurt my loved one at the fatal hour—
        "The mother of their human, buried God!"—
hoping thus badly to unseal by word
        a nugatory free or purple hour
(then from the golden east the zephyrs borne
        meet greyer western vehicles at morn
where an Aurora decks her gleaming hood
        enduring freedom for the general good:
there from the sounding base was heard afar
        the noise of aircraft longing for the war

The Unconditional

to which succeeding charitable drops
        bomb with all help available in shops
yet lighter task to stay the angry waves
        than to set one stop on the westered graves
whose seas unknown and foreign regions lost
        wish to spill open careless of the cost
until Jerusalem in prospect lie
        letting its dismal armies flare and die.
Where no contrition saddens any breast
        and holy sorrow goes down with the rest
while practiced tongues a perfect speech supply
        sealing discomfort with a stony eye.
So undistinguished murmurs fill the air
        where neither mingled joy nor grief appear.
So when bare desert cooling gales receives
        no slightest noise is heard among no leaves.
So to a deaf man standing by the shore
        the hollownesses of the billows roar.
Each throws his martial ornaments aside
        for casual grit delivered nationwide.
In cheerful shirtsleeves for the evening news.
        In a matte metal for the killing cruise.
So at the close of every working day
        work clothes to leisure pastels shall give way.

The Unconditional

So when a frozen heart the very ground
        on which its saviour's passing death was found
refuses peremptorily to weep
        sticking instead inside its bony keep
but stores up all its unexpended tears
        for small defeats and narcissistic fears
then a small creature's pitiable blood
        may come consoling to release the flood:
and who watched murders cheering on for more
        can yet convulsively a mouse deplore.
Now like a whirlwind rushing through the skies
        swift information through the ether flies
whose name had never been at all remade
        since raging clients wrote the first crusade
while poets of our day by much prefer
        the exculpated victim in fake fur
thus by a light skip disinhabiting
        the capital I cannot choose but sing
("Go then again transfiguring to fate
        all the inedible bad meals you ate.
You 'cannot choose' but munch another's flesh,
        too gladly caught in 'nexus' or in 'mesh'.
So when Persephone negated best
        forms not no subject of a Christian song

The Unconditional

nor Pelops with his bitter friendly gifts
        nor from Dodona the loquacious oak
nor the armed dances of a weeping god
        not not escaping from his father's hate
are not lamented nor purgated then
        and more too shameful still to be described
is also not-described in counterpoint
        diminishing a dim ship to a dot
loved and deflected into lustrous dark
        still more illustrious as more crossed with love
or ever into eyeless foundering
        decapitated idols yawning grief
in long litotes make a sad parade
        of underwater colours where the bark
beleaguered in an allegory bobs
        frail and unsinkable toward its port
light as Carthusian skiff of Ursula
        laden with masses rosaries and prayers
upon which passengers might freely draw
        while over them as spiritual sail
eleven thousand paternosters sped
        that boat to heaven over the grey Rhine
whose well lit waters covering Hörsel there
        require we sink her worshipped image-ship

The Unconditional

and drown all idols in oblivion where
        by dissolution they the true craft bear
up on the thick meniscus of this world:
        from whom you rather should take hint for flight
striking for once in life a cheerful note
        or slip for once then off your lighter coat
sooner than gaze into the lovely deep
        you yourself colour with the greenest sleep
yet call this lure society or fate
        prepersonating there a fatal sea
whose salt light air laughs off your lending voice
        to dance in finite possibility
while from a drip you feed the general good
        drying the ocean up to give it food.
Bury the whole Adam in the water then!
        Only from drowning suck your natal breath!
Lest when the light goes out across the street
        illumination exiting the world
remember daylight only in a book
        still re-deleted from the user-base
this story lost forever to your brain.
        Naked but armed in Christ fifteen years old
revulsing from the crowds who gathered there
        from the no-city in the desert he

how much too liable to be overcome
	walking in rustic cloak toward the swamp
enjoyed that vast and terrible solitude.
	Feeding on fifteen figs before the sun.
Haircut once a year for the resurrection.
	Purest in unwashed for a holy crust.
Soon he was 63 years old.
	"Plagued by the crowds on my first ever world tour
raging with kindness to revenge myself
	I scourge them with an instancy of prayer
while ever while I meditate on flight
	and how my grave is best to be concealed
lest a dog patron dig it up and build
	a chapel over it or other such
I for the cattle pastures keenly long
	since only fiercest enemies are there
best loving me who hate my carcass best."
	"Many in England think you must be mad.
But Brindley too did his best work in bed.
	Pink then and lilac quivering in haze
we to ourselves must image out your top
	of telescopic clarity in sky
flaming as scarlet painted on the blue
	your iron bridges of seclusion bore."

The Unconditional

"Perhaps. I prayed incessantly. I wept.
        I tore my flesh. This stony world slid off
from regions of undying adamant
        interior to my hiddenness itself.
Craving no sea but chucked into the drink
        emerging wet and baptized like a fool
just falling backwards into perfect bliss." ")
        when one least turning of the fated earth
could even now release the world from dearth
        stripping its violence from the working day
as common light may fall along the way
        the squad flew glutting scouring and to strow
discriminating fire on those below
        while all across the plain its yells were heard
and by them to a different sense referred.
        Over all devastated vacuums there
no living speaker could gulp no good air.
        Over the spick rehygienated void
(a nil by enmity quite unalloyed)
        perfect impossibility was seen
of visible bloodshed from the good machine
        since furies gently tucked up there in bed
all warlike word that ever might be said
        in sentence wanting badly to let out

The Unconditional

some really present bad delight or shout
        as of the concentrated hatred where
aching for some revenge Clorinda there
        sigh weep or rage her metal coat to bits
longing to rain on Tancred bloody hits
        until the vizors in a smashing kiss
rend with a shriek that barrier to bliss
        leaving his pale and her still paler face
open and weakening in that empty place
        where from torn metal only now will burst
these golden tresses banishing the worst
        declaring sex and all else to the world
where thought of harm to outer darkness hurled.
        Each insult stopping in the other's mouth.
Each dumb north melting into speaking south.
        Each limb caresses changing there for blows.
Each soulless impulse for the soul it knows.
        Each cool deflection changed for open hurt.
Each cruel reflection for a hopeless blurt.
        Thus while they mingle all desiring limbs
mangling no others' with sententious hymns
        —for other's others' others are the Same
where indistinguishable bliss pertains—
        as when a huddled gloom of vestibule

The Unconditional

placed at the opening to a Residenz
        gives of ecclesiastic purple not one glimpse
bending the royal neck to stoop inside
        and forcing through the smallest entrance there
a train which slowly mounts the sweep of stair
        head down to marble till some filament
into the corner of the dormant eye
        drop there one grain of unattended light
pulling the neck with a sharp tug back to tilt
        so the whole face falls open then and up
the mouth must slacken following the eye
        burst from its stillness by the open blue
pale as a painted morning sky from which
        incomprehensibly suspended there
floating with all ease into middle air
        cruel Barbarossa and five hundred horse descend
offering tumbrils to the vacant head
        and with no other force than this éclat
land mortal monarchs flat out on their backs.
        So there subjunctives imperceptibly
change for indicatives their let this be
        waking to know for a small instant pain
until the soothing rota sound again
        its reassuring daily cruelties.)))))

and we will gape to see the folk fall out
        in bloody patterns on the impassive screen)
making it hardly possible to think
        more than with memory of clutch and gears
embedded in his fumbling hands and feet
        which since surrendering immortal gas
split by a lung or backbone Agramant
        now found the cleverest left part of him
working like rusted auto parts which yet
        have some more miles to go before they fail
unlike his muddled head which lunged and grabbed
        with useless imprecision for the point
of following this hardly visible blur
        of blue or purple off into the far
and dim proximities of Cambridgetown
        and barely had recovered competence
before a felt lament assailed his ear.
        "O second family I cannot love
whose colleagueliest affection kills.
        The second family never known to love
is cunning rancour in the pudding spills.
        Warfare the first profession leaves its brand
in every second family sans blood
        just as the first initiation wounds for good

The Unconditional

and so by hurting sets thus well apart
        vocationally dedicate to death
an isonomically levelled square
        delineating mortal justice where
hired mourners and hired poets advertize
        loss of the loss which cost them more than all
since losing loss they merely decorate
        the flagged floss topping of the warlike state.
An insect march struts on like breath warmed up
        in every paid department of a life
trilling its health-vocation soberly
        from firm fair-minded hatreds in the face
to any living thing we scour with grace
        who every lunchtime at the fatal games
hymn and pre-bury our bloodthirsty names.
        O second family I cannot love
professionally exfoliating good
        that one good man or Man-or-woman jump
happy as Larry to a fatal smash.
        Then carry me to Abraham I pray.
Whose bosom tenderly shelters and refreshes
        all the once spared sons running to death.
I crave am hold lamb in solvents."
        Meanwhile another lump of pudding travelled down

the loose oesophagus into the trunk.
        Concerts of library trolleys all trilled back
the same irregular refrain in squeaks
        shaped like ensemble work recalling the
excessively amused forever damned
        chorus of demons from the underworld
arranged in Guildford Theatre's best shot
        at operettas of Jacques Offenbach
Oh yes! Oh yes! He crave am hold the lamb
        Oh yes! in glutinous solutions-O!
imploding while with desperate resolve
        the audience hung on every single word
knowing that hell was hardly less at hand
        in thoughts and details of the coffee hour
than in the interview or the exam
        as to themselves they pleasantly revolved
the memorabilia of easy death
        from page to page the soothing programme long
and from the cooler gardens at the back
        a *Fantasia sopra Crispin Cobbler* came
(on Crispin "kiss my arse or no vote from me"):
        "Confused by the slipperiness of culture codes
the artisan employs his body to subvert them.
        And in the absence of a textual countercode

The Unconditional

this rude rough music was his only choice."
        Then warbled half-note sociologica
helpfully rush in to supply the same
        fluting as loudly as the stick would go
to unconceal effaced particulars
        which vicious claims for fluting had erased
occluded buried and elided there
        ("Crispin O see with undeluded flutes
we now come to your aid 'gainst flautists!")
        Crispin employed his body to subvert them
with Honest gumption socking in the face
        as glad subchoruses of unemployed
poets and painters cheered the good man on
        hoping it was not them next for the chop
and weakly offering instead to sell
        copies at cut price of the usual rag
printed and thought of on the premises
        here in neither Washington nor Moscow.
Agramant felt numb from the neck up.
        He had completely lost sight of $=x$.
Stumbling straight out into the massive fields
        he felt the freezing rain with all relief
drop on his useless head from the big sky
        wishing for death like every other man

and still unable to discern his wish
        like any other particle of mud
nourished to failure with a careful hand
        and quite incapable of vomiting
the chemicals donated to its gut.
        In brilliant grey in grey the luminous
redundancies of a perpetual rain
        patrolled the enormous acreages there
consoling him with insignificance
        and thus competing for the hipflask's job
in who should find the first true quick oblivion.
        The lowing cattle-objects could not weep.
The dog ran howling from the addict sheep.
        The baby beats the nurse up with a frown.
Refrain: *Against nature*, etc. x 8 to close.
        Agramant began to feel a lot better.
Removing from selected large wild pigs
        the top incisor thus encouraging
the bottom tooth to start to curve around
        and then at length to make a circle there
or sometimes even two or three full wheels
        of dental artifice the helpless pigs
were now incapable of finding food and so
        Agramant fed them with his own white hand

The Unconditional

anticipating with a hardening glee
        rococo tooth-transporters when they oink
drovered by Agramant himself across
        the desert set-asides of Anglia
into the squawking combination rooms
        of outraged modernism would at once
send to oblivion with their toothy trump
        of long accumulated soul-stuff all
the feeble onlookers as then and there
        the slaughtered beasts would distribute their gules
reddening the Cam with irrefutable
        brightest self-evidence of artifice
and all their dentistry incorporate
        in bone of Agramant at his own skull
with force of passionate conviction thus
        magnanimously crushing epigones
then sauntering off to the pub to enjoy it properly.
        Their names home to him like a flock to north.
Later in Services formica teemed.
        Nonsemiotic grapefruit-eating all about
extended its impossible ideal.
        Lay your knife and your fork across your plate.
Against all furious effort the slack face
        still with each gobful let some wet sign slip

to sit with meaning on the grating chin
        while if de minimis a muscle there
could give no noticeable twitch that did
        not paint a message in the vacant air
causing nonsemiosis to migrate
        from off this world's bad grapefruit to some skies
of uninhabitable scientistic loss.
        Agramant tucked into his bacon.
The surfaces were decked with fragments of a meal
        eaten before him and resistibly
recalling undistinguished epochs in the life
        or afterlife of sundry modernisms since
detritus first had come into its ownmost truth
        now with no lesser weight upon this top
of mind-erasing furniture to sit
        inimitably organizing here
with greasy cunning the entire sad hole
        kindly conceding to the junior tribes
some passing clouds of possibility
        gripped and extinguished for the next degree show.
Still the wet grapefruit dribbled out a song.
        In this story only the experiences are true.
Unknowing time drops off like the broke ghost.
        Yellow and green as the parts of a sky

The Unconditional

fringing the tonic | dominant of red
        and orange booming out their foolish wish
so were the partial scraps of citrus stuck
        on to the stubbled desert of a jowl
stretching with more than deathly less than life-
        (or two-) faced pallor over the tired bone
presented to him over table which
        delightful horror creeping on his skin
began to intimate across slow bits
        or fractions of the breadthless depthless line
immeasurably indivisible to points
        yet none the less consisting of such points
each which dimensionlessly was construed
        as each the absolute unconditional now
each so acute a zenith as to impale
        citated human subjects on its point
experiencing nothing at this x
        and totalling by help of spasming limbs
into a failed embrace each one of each
        to make up all the meaning of a life
before in perfect corpuscles of time
        Agramant could begin to recognize
across the table from him that thin $=$x.
        he had assumed was at the pole by now.

The Unconditional

As leopardseals who when the film crews sail
        past their best hunting grounds put on a show
and also when there are no film crews there
        put on a show too but not so described
(the show residing only in the stuff
        verbal support teams bring up from the rear)
and sometimes twenty minutes can elapse
        between the point at which the prey first bleeds
and that at which the second bite goes in
        so Agramant with fearful pleasure makes
a slight delighted slump of his right shoulder
        as he soon feels the supplementary air
reoxygenating all his sleepy blood
        and innerly reflects with glee on how
the heavenly endorphins once thought lost
        revive from out the caverns of the soul
and then remembers to revise this glee
        instantly crossing out the thought of soul
replacing it with category-mistake
        and praying to the outraged endorphins there
not to cut out and thus to make all room
        for all reflection shrink down to a dot
the sole condition of whose sponsorship
        is freedom from metaphysics in continuums

The Unconditional

of matter pleasurably in a middle voice
        subsisting in the manner of a smile
spreading from ear to ear without more sense
        of subject or of object than the sky
or than a tiny and malicious gene
        economistically 'acting' 'in'
'its' 'own' 'self' 'interest' in a novel by
        Sir Richard Dawkins Baronet of Slush
where all the characters have gone to sleep
        in imitation of the author's mind
which he himself says cannot be awake
        in broader daylight than a stick of rock.
So did delight roll all through Agramant
        just as his perfectly impassive face
or so near perfect as leaves scarce a breath
        of signifying matter on its skin
hardened by one iota in its joy
        pushing a little burst of used air from his lungs
and through the mouth shaped in the form of this
        "Hi." A little space of time just sat up cute.
A miniature universe of fun
        between the dawning of the instant when
the sun of recognition came first up
        in pinks and purples of uncertainty

The Unconditional

inside the optic nerve of 'poor' =x.
        And when it set again through burning clouds
in certain knowledge that his enemy
        was sitting there in service station blue
as when first rumour of a coming war
        from crevices in mute intelligence
leaks to the avid wire or wireless beam
        a possible integer of probable
risk or then hope dividing from the fold
        brushes against the oil price like two lips
on the most sensitive no skin there is
        the slightest contact more than nothing will
call up all spirits from their surfaces
        sending all shocks of terror or delight
whether to eros or to thanatos
        or operatives to their sleepy screens
jerk on to power up the data field
        setting the eddying hammering of blood
as a no wave on no field spends its flood
        whose figures bear away a man's whole life
by one dead jump into the real sea
        whilst they caress the exquisitely keen
crest which falls off to pleasure or to pain.
        So =x. drowned down in ripeness.

The Unconditional

A space which offered views and promenades
        to Agramant who strolled on the parterre
arranging eye-catchers at salient points
        where round the corner of a wooded path
you turns and is at once hailed by a plinth
        or absolutist obelisk in jest
whose joke much more sadistic than it knows
        wishes to finish off the client past
lording with indefeasible capital
        all properties of the still vanquished gods
pushing beneath the christian tarmac there
        all wires and pumps of demonized since fair
illuminated metamorphosed sprites
        anticipating drop of equals x
into self-praising ha-has of the brain.
        More on this later.
Just as the possible mage had drawn the plan
        of that estate a slow tongue just crawled up
out of the back of '=x.' mouth to say "Oh hi."
        "Hi" then accompanied small convulsive nods
as though of greeting or of welcome bobbed
        from off the neck-top with elastic dumb
"where are you off to then" attempting to
        repeat failed grapefruit trick of say gar nichts

The Unconditional

by saying something so as to displace
        all thought of Reals in that possible place
wanting to smash his enemy in the face
        wanting to still be nice to everyone
so nothing nasty ever would occur
        or nothing at all ever but defer
hoping at last cold Agramant would then
        answer the question and release again
from obligation of initiative
        his saddened throat and tongue which stuck back down
in face of mage's terrifying smile
        and powerful belly pushing off the beach
much worse than any blow expelling him
        to the last regions of recorded crime
where in erasure every part of skin
        did crumple ceaselessly and hope for death
thus summoning his every worst of sin
        in recollection of immeasurable
ill by himself committed to the good
        pushing him backwards off his tipping chair
smiled to the ground by simple ridicule
        helped to his feet with still more modest grin
and good kind clammy hand explaining him
        to be the extremest slime that ever coats

The Unconditional

earth's superficies with pernicious dirt
        as "thank you, thank you" puttered from
his grapefruit-sputtered wobbling-weeping chin
        "thank you so much" "Goodbye!" This grave return
sounded from back of head as Agramant'
        s face headed boldly through the door
preoccupied unable to express
        perfect psychosis as genetic code
and peering with a horrid glimmer in
        to the quite sickening awareness that
other and other breaths must yet be drawn
        if merely to remember this one peak
of utterly successful happiness
        and doubting then with real nausea that
even a smashed and broken $=x$.
        must be again resmashed without all end
merely to stop himself from throwing up.
        Ten miles off ten fat ducks sat on a lake.
Ten thousand miles away the forest floor
        could patiently allow all animals
to clamber over every part of her.
        The stones of one Dalmatian city could think more
than any particle in either skull.
        Washes of air leak through an open window.

The Unconditional

Recovering himself to fantasy
        =x. split up then into the bit to float
and bit to give up over to the fire
        then split that bit into the pure and waste
thus floating twice the floated part of him
        into an element of destiny
which twice in vain re-un-resecularized
        got him at least from table to the door
in good enough shape not to fall to floor
        staggering to the car and falling in
grasping first bottle and then a small book
        he clutched into his tightening wet grip
and as the sobs diminished reconvoked
        his scattered forces to a final stand
remembering how one previous crise morale
        had been averted by a single throw
of broken spirit to unfeeling stone
        when countertransferences had begun
with smallest messengers of terror in
        his barely sentient ear for it to say
that T. was leaving him not before time
        yet in this early period the hues
were rose and blue still of eventual end
        prewarning only by small dissonance

The Unconditional

heard in a growing incapacity
        to keep a face straight in the tearoom when
some simple factual question there addressed
        a vacancy straight opening in his cheek
and twitching Liar with its honest mad
        returning and bespeaking gram of flesh:
then by one lucky page turn landing in
        a sentence of improbable extent
to ferry him across the Lido where
        the congeries of stones was there declared
to exact each from his prebaffled stare
        the same attention as whole authorships
and with the same chance of retaining truth
        or rather more than many libraries
and best of all to be indifferent to
        the absoluteness of his present lapse
made emblems in unemblemable place
        resolved to take a sortilegium
on *Grace Abounding to the Chief of Sinners*
        whose quick gematriot when totted up
could be interpreted at once to call
        for a diversion via Peterborough.
The boarding house he fortunately found
        afforded just the palatable damp

The Unconditional

he hardly dared to hope for on the walls
        and just recalling at its lip of dankness the
bare feeling of the real in general
        he switched the radio on at once to talk
which made a dwelling place of whispered news
        while leafing idly through the Ignatian page
he for experiment or so he said
        to the thick residue of his father's voice
positivistically scorning all
        that smelt of papist metaphysics and
resounding still inside his hyper-I
        turned heart and soul where he imagined them
to be located to this one attempt
        framed or ameliorated by the wallpaper
in Sandersons Chinoiserie 1963
        where silhouetted junks did lazily
in portage of protected fantasies
        of oriental timelessness float down
some turbid flood plain of the bedtime tale
        as from the world tonight the hushed reports
could murmur comforts of the dead and sick
        their silver greys all counterposed with red
and ochre golds of foliage or of bank
        while oxen shaping towards ideograms

he then late knew to be the very stuffs
> just as that quality of sentience did
as metaphysic fiction consciousness
> begin to drop or switch off from the head
which once had made up the entire large wall
> next to his bed in homeliest counties or
as the quick concept grip began to blur
> and in far distance noise of starting trains
destined for Yarmouth and the Suffolk coast
> awoke with one jarred rail a memory
of a town square surrounded by its shops
> each with the same sign set for fifty years
like modern living well repainted up
> once every decade with more pathos when
sans serif pastels age and then renew
> as the same fashion items come back true
and Paris Girl adjusts a headscarf still
> while forward-looking mannequins may gaze
with deadly concentration through the glaze
> to chasten retro with a lighter grace
holding that open which no salve may heal
> as unreal green, that herald of the spring
just lifts an eyelid or sets off a ring
> (sirens of self oblivion, whose least glint

gives to weak poets the worst kind of hint:
        who hugs a polycarapace along
at the fresh feel of this neglected song
        tomorrow dresses windows with his guts
stripped of all cushions' ironizing buts
        (I powerlessly amble through the night
while each new footfall models in unfree
        restrained deceleration half of me.
In what new puddle shall I place my shoe
        whose toecap twiddles its andante through
chiasmic voyages from chair to door
        and door to chair or back again to top
forced to be me free to return and sit
        deferring glory to the other bit
which in perpetual store of window light
        believes prosthetically for me when
I nod or snore my firm convictions then
        counting all night by proxy up to ten))   55/1
thus near enough to sound but far to drift
        in ambiguities of possible meaning which
just as in Catholic pianism I
        so in some hushed fine dogma passage will
thanks to the microphone's embeddedness
        on framework of the instrument awake

immeasurable sonorities decay
        over some several seconds while I wait
the next doctrinal or instructive chord
        hearing the wood with what unearthly voice
declare a music which I only hope
        was thus intended by the catenist
as of the former railway underground
        crescendos like an ondes martinot
or rather as that moment when the strings
        silence their best reverberations we
in spite of technical proficiency
        hear in the street accelerating cars
hushed to truth almost by the thick stone walls
        while though I sleep my heart is still awake
looking at baby Jesus twenty times
        he thought or then imagined and he dreamt
how circling to the zenith of one rock
        suggested by *some* light touch of the brush
which in one vertical could there connote
        a castellated series on the slope
which half awake he half interpreted
        combining with it half Loyola's skill
or half of half as he began to drowse
        the castle No Such Thing to which he crawled

across a river which a textbook told
        was named No Transcendental Signified
and beating down no gates of nothing there
        he came into a hospitable hall
where he was greeted with the image of
        a courtesy which 'never did exist'
in any corner of the storied earth
        yet which was always fabled all the more
it always 'failed to have existed' since
        it always failed to not-exist as well
placing with indiscoverable skill
        a small bound volume in his spirit hands
which seemed to him the clearest sense of all
        redacting in his thinking-thinking sleep
printed catenas unrepeatably
        enshrining and betraying a unique
delivered instance of performance there.
        EPHPHATHA |
Treatise of inarbitrable perdition. |
        [4 lines of Syriac verse. Dedication.] |
Issued from Deptford by the editor |
        now first translated into all the tongues. | | |
The three ideas of the lost
        Ageless hear and thus unlost

The Unconditional

Summa rhythmica which blare
        Perfect doctrine from your mask
Bolt down music to this task.
        Saryngx which I ever bear
Beating hard inside the ear
        Credit athletes of the past
Knowledgeless in every fear
        Still in foolish script at last
With the record which we are.
        Vocatives which chant bereft
Hoping quickly to be left
        By the loyal workers far
Starving on the golden ore
        Do you idly now redraft?
Minus grandeur where you laughed
        Do you classify your more
Instrumental new redress
        As abstraction from the less
Real surface of a thought
        Lacking the wooden stuff it ought
If to confirm ought more than loss
        Would at all make good all loss?
Do you threaten every harm?
        Do you murder? You discharm?

The Unconditional

Do you alter every law?
        Do you lie? Do you disarm?
Do you hollow each new thought
        Out from a concave equals x
Then to a theory just add sex
        Or no better than you ought
Precirculating all the reft
        Dried components of a lack
Biographize an atom where
        No place to live no life comes back
To no first last or middle there?
        Truth to tell I now cohere
Correspond and-or only
        Co-speak when spoken to or
Count up to seven dead.
        One two three four five six.
Still grammatically share
        Majuscules retained I ask
Lest those minuscules should bask
        On the fabric which they tear
From the drapery of past
        Cruelty their lushest peer
Outwards to oblivion's last.
        Glimmering to azures free

Best constrained where without fear
        Dead to immortality
All autumnal commandeer
        Crumble the laureates bereft
Screening hope in the shrill poor
        Last they buy the morning star.
Last they by the morning star
        What thin ray of light is shed
Never struck with wondering eye
        More than with its concepthood
Where from its place without a why
        Sodium glares repel all sight
Of all light other than this loss
        Navigate no earthly course.
Dumb tour de force.
        Panparatactical evade
All speculative violence
        Of the Idea which may not fade
However hard it prays to sense
        Preferring whiteness to the black
Key of pointed syntax whence
        The sky receives all meant and felt lack.
Metafeeling shuts up shop.
        Beauty in the clinic.

Exclamations never dare
        Fearing classifying task
Or as abstract still recask
        Ever to speak their first names there
Servile plugging up the ear
        Shunning stoppages or fast.
All the top extremes I grab
        With superlative unfree
Deaf to poor mortality
        Colour my failure frozen red.
Life's blood won't from that ice.
        Live grub rips to shred
That trumped up twice.
        Goodness knows.
Half waking from this severated sleep
        $=x$. half fell back again into the deep
water of half gone semisentience
        or fell far back enough to note down then
the textual supplements crammed into the back.
        "The long transmission history of $=x$
leaves many matters quite insoluble.
        No manuscripts survive. The princeps stems
from poor translations into Punic Latin made
        in those quotations from our F which surface in

The Unconditional

the Montanist polemics against F.
        Those works themselves are lost. A Nitrian saint
in the decaying ages of the cells
        when few or none could muster any wish
to do more than keep codices from sale
        gave his exulting miseries to this
job of recovering all scraps of F
        which he collated in a work thought lost
which later happening to be unearthed
        by some assistants of Richard Simon
were circulated in a Latin text
        while the originals were once more lost.
What we have have we only from the pen
        of a commercial traveller who had
in course of real breakdown found some help
        in innocent amusements of this kind
translating short of polished elegance
        which English had afforded by this date
all the known shards of F into such verse
        as could be mustered from his Lettish ear."
=x. could not believe a word of this romance
        reverting instantly with half his brain
to the too comically transparent source
        in the 'lost' essay of Wilamowitz

on the 'much troubled' textual history
> Manilius bequeathed to after time

and as he snored there to a purpose still
> resolving in his dream to (next) complete

a census of the copies of princeps
> capitulating all his little hope

into the superstition that some catch
> or ligature might finitely betray

an absolutely other history
> of loss and emptiness behind this work

which with dry weeping of that only kind
> which comes in our few elegiac dreams he saw

had mentioned him by name line 36
> and thus proposed a practicable course

confiding his no destiny to this task
> despite repugnant similarity

to job description of wine critic still
> refusing critical editions yet

in dissertations clearly setting out
> the human knowledge relevant to F

interring passion in that residence
> of unimpeachable pure labour which

bore in procession the stuffed effigy
> of work before it dried into a ghost

since what as he began to wake he saw
        was how much the idea of perfect loss
(where 'perfect' means eventuality
        of total and immitigable lack
of some one thing or thought once made or felt
        or of some utter indeniable
experience deleted from all mind)
        in its obstruction to the castors of
all trolley-borne descriptivism did
        much more than any plenitude retain
the general note of real blessedness.
        It was already next week.
A white building for hundreds of metres.
        A white cuboid with some eyelets.
A white area hundreds of square metres.
        Face no face but for its no eyes.
All are as vulgar where not understand.
        So awe leaks from my sleepy mouth.
Delight most bold most unavailable
        as though one of the treu constructivists
too good to be remembered in this world
        and perfectly forgotten from the shop
had left some single monument of stone
        translated from an early canvas here

to this aggressively retreated slab
        of middle western agribusiness land
and then had spent the years of exile here
        sculpting a metal tag 5 in by 3
with the decisive logo into blue
        perpetually signifying there
the reason of the interlocking spheres
        of influence shed by invisibles
zoo logo echo to perimeters
        where this impossible ineffable
true or untrue concern begins to fringe
        a hypothetically charted way.
A thin and shining path of tarmac walks
        in imitation of a public road beside
that indecipherably seeming fair
        head quarters of a not to be known host.
Kilometres of fences run along
        accompanying with their passagework
deflected majesties of candid blank
        denied and celebrated grandest notes
because the highest art is truly paid
        by capital which modestly conceals
the good it always does with the left hand
        I write good with no irony at all

preparing for the no spectators this
        ruthlessly theoretical new lawn
some tens of metres wide and hundreds long
        which I would still have measured but for those
too commentitious fences at the side
        preventing me from walking on the grass
like the alarms surrounding Malevich
        except more quite retired into a depth
interinscannable by any eye
        which would take at face value all the face
put up there for Imperial Industries
        as this firm trust was now no longer named
doffing its despots to the written east
        welcoming no republics to the west
and thus more powerful than any one
        supposed authentic feeling in my head
wanting too stupidly to take for real
        power growing with the weight weight power
head shrinking with the light of powerful
        imperial barbiturates obtained
at cost from inside on a sponsorship
        yet never able to do more to grass
than shave it back to the precise extent
        at which still grass it carpets out the space

The Unconditional

personing inside-outside on a space
        500 x 300 pinned and mapped
pages of doctrine in the form of grass
        destructing patiently all dual truth
cutting the inside from the outside where
        it grew yet not grew, nor a plant nor text
but very element of inside-out
        ness nailed out more than sacrificially
with violenceless domestic openness
        made for no human sole to brush and feel
but still incorporate inhuman role
        into renaturated culturings
of preacculturated nature where
        the boundaries were blurred by regiments
of still obedient subversives there
        mowing the lawns in holist paragraphs
past groups of pronouns drawing up their plans
        to run on and pick up the lyric tab.
Money mourn Person from its metal tree.
        "My long discolouration is well known.
Well known how I lost gratifying charm
        from old successes swiftly rising up
to general equivalence and death
        rendering me pliable as clods of clay

to bear the crowned heads of the falling world
        thus advertizing to the guillotine
their promisingly absent necks in gold
        or usually in alloy or some such.
O Money, Money, beat at this headless lump
        tinnily to lament My own decline
by apotheosizing t-i-n
        beyond the sociable collision in
po-po-politest arbitrariness."
        "Push what falls over down the quickest shute.
Be on the right side of whatever comes.
        Be right as rain proclaiming irreversible
the stomach contents of inhabitants
        of tabulated morgues across the state.
Be absolute in cutting out the part
        that badly wishes for its dummy back.
Off with its head I say and let us all
        think the more freely with the gushing stump!"
Person mourn Money immaterially.
        The hundred dollars ceases to exist.
It is not contradictory at all.
        It was the best funeral choir this side of hell.
It ought to be, look at the invoice.
        Just as each neuro-sector tub turn-takingly

may from a poison expertise expire.
   So each potential readership is stripped
by insults well administered in time."
   "You've got it bad. Hilariously I must
just break up with a giggle at your lust
   always to hit upon the classic tweeds.
Bonny Count Sacher-Masoch get down now.
   The king over the water listen is the last
most sherry-sodden protest of the kid
   milking the taxpayers for every least
complaining blether from its Age of Bleat.
   Worship your paycheck in that tartan drag
while I respond to relevant demands.
   Nothing but your rage is left of you.
Your mouth is opened only to give pain.
   If you succeed, the credit is not yours
but only that we see your sum of hate.
   Hoping that vehemence alone will float
your leaden commonplaces through one more
   interminable seminar you crawl
crabwise through brown decanters to what end.
   Oh sorry 5 x 2 that must be some
apotropaic recipe you mean.
   Blub to your oak tree sooner than to me.

And don't expect a receipt."
    The listeners hymned a silent good amen
thanking their lucky stars that they had learnt
    themselves to put away all irony
with other toy prostheses in a box
    of all outgrown deflections they now dropped.
Yet one doubt still lisped limpid to a lip.
    "Deflection shelter in some case the true.
A lyric gesture from the stomach floor
    ejecting unexperience of nil
distributed remediably knows
    better than real self-cutting how the skin
promotes abstraction when it falls asleep.
    Dismiss my soul, where no carnation fades."
Autosottisier, fill my stupid boots.
    Batrachomyomachially I
sing every foolish false foot well above
    the bottom line of debit into cold.
=x. first stopped the car and then got out.
    Sometimes the other way round is best.
So this is what Allegory, Nebraska looks like.
    That must be the post office.
Anything can stand for anything else.
    Horizonlessly off into the grey

The Unconditional

an infinite grisaille kenotically
        prevacating all shades to substance churns
unconscious of the universal truth
        that substance grins its core of essence in
known only for its superficies there
        where substances are reckoned up by dog
hoovering through the grades of qualities
        three-headed nominally hungry beast
until a single plane slides off and out into
        the all indifferentiable sky
whose clouds conformed themselves to letters there.
        "We clouds refute the work of Walter Benn Michaels."
=x. turning with revulsion from the grey
        or hyperpedagogical sublime
turning with equal shudder from the maw
        of common-reader-masks worn by the dataplug
turned finally with equal horror from no self
        able to save him from the after-bild
of Agramant demolishing with smile
        every last cell of self-sufficing joy
cornered against time over time in his
        good evenings when he put aside his cares
and would read Livy in his fresh clean robes
        or other rational pleasures of dismay

The Unconditional

in sober satisfaction crawling on
        in sober desperation nearly gone
unable to forget that knowing face
        peering so gaily into helpless guilt.
By wandering we go to not not right.
        Thickets of error overgrow the right.
As great a miracle it is to see
        the weight of sin which makes the souls recoil
from a true centre into open pain
        suspended capable of good and still
as to see rocks in the forgetful air
        refusing still their own desire to rush
into the heart of gravity or good
        retaining insubstantial free despair
as satellites may orbit out of air.
        =x. ran in terror from his body there.
He had to get back home straight away
        in order to reconstruct the lost notebooks
reharbouring the needful emblems which
        had been restolen from his inner lounge.
Storied in acetate a burgundy
        or mock-reptilian texture dinosaured
it to the top possible lush risible
        extent of decor in a modern cell

begging for damp or other quisling who
   might leak those fibres to the country air
but always miserably fortified
   with all acculturated plastics where
the very idea of nature always was
   killed off by indoor plants triumphally
hymning pansemiosis from their pots.
   You have to be changed into rain to get in.
As soon as you are in you want to die.
   The first warm canape which circulates
brings to its comic knees the mixed Idea.
   The first smart joke expiring on his lips
at once pre-beckons up a spectral train
   of trowels and headstones juggling with skulls.
Then write that these jokes just are what there is.
   Declare his toxic cocktail cabinet
to be no less the essence of the world
   than any other mere phenomenon
while the best elegists in the whole bad loop
   restate their shattering laments once more.
Dragging his title Self out of this drain
   =x. heard sang voices to himself from top.
"Throw yourself into your work.
   Then from the deep as on a string will bounce

back with a surplus every coin you drop.
        "Throw your work away.
Then listen closely to your life of loss
        knowing no other hears so well as you
specific contours of that long descent.
        "You are thrown down.
Strive to receive the shape of being nil.
        Throwing throws all your projects in the bin.
Log it at least you honourably can.
        "Thrown up and out rather why do you
still think you at all think in this bone or
        do ought but delete with all efforts at
write or record or think your honour less?
        You're going to catch it."
"Yes." Yes." Yes." Yes. Throw – catch. Throw – catch. Two more.
        Your name is ready for you in the bag.
Pull it on over your head and in each pouch
        let your desiring-knowing-suffering stuffs
name substance subject and be free to force
        their multiplicitous and single voice
down other throats like that it leaps up from.
        Practical parenting retrumpet now
a vale of subject-making garlanded
        with all the exiled saints and demons who

The Unconditional

pushed from the office must take up their home
        in simulacra of the Children's work
guarding a choir which yet can lift no voice
        ever or ever audible above
the em pathetically caring drone
        of all key workers well concerted there
addressing through that infant frontispiece
        some Parents huddled in a darkened room
bound in collective judgement to the front
        an undertow of solidary love
is still remembered and the look and tone
        minute breaks in the face then blurting
taking time off from work to see our son
        mutely perform by singing through the eyes
hoping above all else to go back home
        transferring thus in mental book-keeping
from sale to gift or clock into surprise
        status to contract forces to be free
all that gratuitously leaps from me
        in perfect spontaneity and truth
co-ordinated here on two hand helds
        to capture special memories for good
with how monocular benevolence
        from this fair festival of insideout

trained up to hope for nothing but the best
        most adequated interface with nil.
Twinkle then first to catastrophic suns
        nor ask for milk and honey from the sky
raining its stony signals everywhere
        marked BREAD WITH CARE NOT FOR CONSUMPTION down
on the Community of no embrace
        hoping to make the best of sacrifice.
Now climb the stairs by one and one. Good boy
        told to your self and told off from the top
advancing in renunciating light
        administering with care each dose of loss
to trees of macerated paper stood
        with all their bloody logic turned toward
a verdant replica of merely good.
        Learn to eat up the wrapping round my face.
Or stay in your cot for the next forty.
        It's your choice.
                You are Jobless.
He/I broke up the pronoun part of it
        crawling a ward-wards with a dumb or stick
breaking a rule of hear no voices or
        feeling to hear them knowing he should not
let the loose splittle from a corner slip

            out on a chin front giving too much lip
or off his favourite air mandolin
            sketching too vaguely with a limb to show
more than the germ of an idea to
            the key inspector of his concept bank
who with a quick look at the c.v. notes
            obvious nutter in his database
rather of neurones than of bytes made up
            saving his written comments from the light
of irretrievable keystrokes in the dark
            which chief anaesthetician of his age
—I'm going to ask you a few simple questions—
            still would strike Jobless on his lower knee
jerking unhappily to sanity
            a new suit wrapping up what late was there
man with his daughters taken into Care
            terrine of Jobless spruced into a fair
compressed small cake of vegetable stuffs
            in specky competence to grin all Yes
to human abstracts when we would Employ
            peg to a whole as makes all squares go round
remaindering his unfinished monograph
            pre-publication in a fresh advance
in helpful new technologies of loss

The Unconditional

      leaving the waiting world to live to lack
W.T. Krug's Critique of Hegel.
         Jobless's answers to the questionnaire
were wrongly made in verse and follow here.
         "I have them, but I will not give them up.
The one superfluous true book is down
         miles in the earth beneath your feeble care.
Perhaps you do not have them? I have them.
         I have them, but I will not give them up.
"Your boiling lead refreshes us too well.
         Splinters dart backwards from our quicks to stab
who lately pushed them underneath our nails.
         Millstones not drown us but become our rafts
across judicial rivers to the bank.
         Pitch oil and fat may bubble up their best
yet never blemish in the least our skins.
         Then plunge yourself at last out of sheer rage
into the mixture meant for others' harm.
         Clown martyrs killable as rubberized
we meekly now resign our willing necks
         freely surrendering what you could not steal." "
Filled in while waiting for the sportive beam
         to rumble cheesy fanfares over him
at whose first brass note every pen will drop

           and mouth must open slightly while the jaw
relaxes from his usual psycho gritted till
           infinitesimally it descends
letting the tongue once braced for epic loose
           to loll upon a bed of harmless teeth
all mutely chorussing ba-ba-ba-ba
           forming and fading like a half idea
born in homuncular pupils when they dream
           of the light orchestras of Yesteryear
then as this heritage hook fades into an
           insistent thud of classic rock a pulse
ticks three-four faster as the through pass soars
           dispensed from Hull as if to find Brazil
with sympathetic leap the heart dilates
           tracking its every dear digressive move
just as a mazy run bewilders quite
           defenders who at once allegorized
stand stock still like some comic giants there
           creating thus a microsecond where
the meaning of a game is then seized and
           for all the world as though in effigy
the dominated flipped off from the earth
           leaving their masters grasping at thin air
which microsecond shimmers through a crowd

The Unconditional

        curled like a shoal of thinking subjects there
coming as if one to a roar of bliss
        nailed down for ever to the same one grid
still generated punctually there
        where every virtuosic flight of skill
lives for effect off heavy tackles still
        (but as a dominant prepared too long
boils pianistic freedom down from song
        (or as a stolen bit of time-line halts
by quasi imperceptibles for true or false
        (on this side special pleading for the name
plinthed as an extraordinary claim
        with no more freedom than the fated shout
which pre-identifiers will let out
        of acclamation well before the end
of any final note at concert's end
        (longing to be the first to self-approve
with yelling signatures to idol love
        and thus to feel dry waves of clapping back
imaginary baton to the packs
        both singular and representative:
cashing an option both to die and live
        (so will pedestrians hug their inner light
as though their sole proprietary right

The Unconditional

        which all street lighting gathers to secure
binding their freedom to what may endure))
        on that side truly niente but for one
robbed ethically from who does not see
        his whole account diminish by a jot
yet to perception wakes from rêverie
        by just rubato adding to his lot
no substance but a thinking subject who
        returns him interest of six thousand years
(J recollected as the flicker washed
        storms of nonsemiotic light across
non indiscernible identical
        movements of inner facial muscles which
remembered where his brain did not the twitch
        felt when the Letter on Cadenzas first
traversed his synapses with pleasure shocks
        (Dear W;— You spoke last night too well
perhaps to your first topic to attend
        with proper care or earnestness to this:
that what in most you rightly would deplore
        as the bad grab for extra by a limb
wishing to have its cake and eat it too
        (on top of discipline which earns my keep
I invoice for hiatus while you weep)

>   can in one instance hold an aperture
> open inside a monolith of that
>   perduringly identical repeater box
> or long fidelity to all the dead
>   we honour with an iteration's stead
> interring them again with every point
>   we rub from off the session tape and paint
> out with an insert from a second take.
>   What instance is that? When the loco halts
> restrainedly inviting comment from
>   the solo glosser to the inner text
> must we suppose that only he is right
>   who plays the notes in front of him all night?
> There is another possibility.
>   Not self-restrictions chastening a fist
> proposing hardened products heard as live
>   whose exoskeleton may concentrate
> a passing fluid of the merely free.
>   Not the forgiving splatter of *ff*
> or *ppp* at every second breath
>   (a quantity which never ever turns
> to any other quality than burns
>   the whole resource of emphasis to ash
> nor saves one disc from turning into cash)

The Unconditional

        stealing expression only to seal down
the vent of feeling in an abstract frown.
        What is that instance? No example may
(since all examples are a sacrifice
        of the particulars to general twice)
do more than blur the thought for which it longs
        or mar with protocols their sorrows' songs.
Lovers of harmony though heard it shine
        in K. 491 in '48
the obsolescence of whose vinyl corps
        adds exercising inexplicitness
with every surface flaw upon the scale
        unloosing chromatism from its lock
to waver gently out into the air
        of a new planet treading shakily
or as a lamb will wobble on the grass
        so this cadenza lacked all certainty
other than that belief which bears us up
        from one step to the next before we think
how to fall over into earth or drink))))))
        the half completed questionnaire just dropped
into a beer pool where it wetly flopped.
        Spare us the rest of your record collection.
The 'tiny white stick' is a cigarette.

The Unconditional

        J stared from gloom into the Umbrosphere
while in an idling sector of his brain
        some contributions to philosophy
trotted across the synapses unseen
        like too sharp mettle blunted just enough
by opiates wafting from a good cheap suit
        freed thus by worsted worlds to think one thought
more painful than was tolerable when
        by day incarcerated in the street
he walked through infinite concretion where
        no single sphere was more to him than nil
trying to sup deep of its zero air.
        Nothing was hidden from his empty head
who first told every owner of a thought
        to keep it quiet and then told them too
(Reverse of Socrates! to who participates
        in bliss you wrench them back to canning gates)
that speaking language was like playing games
        as from the corner flag a perfect swerve
of disenchanting nominalist curve
        eluded too well schooled defenders' heads
knocking away fans from their dull pin heads
        but only ever had those games in mind
where turns were taken as they were done too

             in disembodied Zeno-classes there
where the polite world's last grim relics sat
             worshipped by the demystified participants
while Zico's free kick billows in the net
             as Jobless lets a lazy foot repose—
paralogistically log into
             my airtight capsule of improper blue
as spilt phlogiston thins the universe
             when lighter by one soul it runs to verse
enjoying twice or not each chance of lunch
             spent backwards in the gap I am to munch.
The gap I am, that absence in the brain
             where thoughts leap sideways in their neural train
in no line solider than soldier ants
             making their plural thought of single chants
which chitinously thinks its dying march
             determinately as a stone or larch—
dug further into carpeting which blazed
             around him utterly outside potential reach
of all attention in its fiery tufts
             of umber and of mandarin or sharp
repulsive yellow sometimes signalled through
             a verdurous polyester at the tip
of certain singular and snot-like tufts

The Unconditional

          recurring 7 cm where
viridous plastic power in points resurged
          recalling artificial Christmas trees
almost entirely buried under weight
          of orange tinsels glowing firily
through which his limbtip bimbled to a stop
          upsetting half a beer can and its glop
refuting thus all languaged theory's mop.
          Jobless too listlessly allowed his eye
to drift like unheld cursor to the top
          whereas a thin strip of the evening sky
3 inches long by 1 deep suddenly
          glimmered a lit mass of illumined cloud
at corner of the screen but half concealed
          by a corona off the anglepoise
hitting the screen too mirrorwise to see
          could none the less not blank out every note
of the four letters which his anxious eye
          made out from several dot of cathode ray
causing a painful tightening at the chest
          or then a lurch up from the lower spine
pushing the head out with its brace of eyes
          to stare down at the flooring which he then
just as the blood arrested in his vein

The Unconditional

        slowly began at that to understand
or feel as though he understood that this
        widely disparaged carpet was a map
of every message which he had to get
        the next ten years or seconds of his life
nothing outside the textile ever spoke
        more forcibly than this of clementine
or muck skip ochres fading to a brown
        then zipped to primrose at occasional
points of most import like the words of Christ
        printed in rubric for the hard of mind
in presentation copies of the word
        distributed at prizegivings but here
shrilling alone a sheer bright lemon thrill
        as at the edge of every nylon spear
a grin like Cadmus almost formed before
        in quasi-letterish dentition leapt
twisting in effortlessly since unwilled
        impish refusal of determinate
recharactering in their every glint
        shining refusal of position since
they in a frenzy burnt a futile course
        between the S and Z cutting a line
whose earthly form upon the carpet there

        perpetually recited silent prayer
now which then J in his belated head
        first rocked him backwards and then left for dead.
We understand each other better now.
        "Only part of language is like chess."
The rainwashed vans and lorries brushing up
        extensive puddles on adjacent roads
every two minutes with their tympani
        touched with the finest care the surface of
a nearly silent medium of air.
        Splash. Wait. Splash. Wait. Splash.
Some few hours later in a pale sunlight
        dropped through the small top window on the floor
an envelope could break its outer chrysalis
        insinuated quaquaversally
from the cocoon of outside world into
        his real flat to get through orifice
brushing its dampened tuft with paper tip
        to drop right down and stay still on the mat.
Jobless' head sideways from his zero bliss
        stared open and as though with living still
dilating and contracting with a palp
        scarcely discernible to human sight
an eye beam still recalcitrantly jumped

The Unconditional

        from the sole letter lying on the mat
back into Jobless' nerveless prostrate fat
        whose indeterminable twitching told
of nothing less than nothing happening
        or something more than something in the thing
just as the pixels brilliantly still
        failing repeatedly to be switched off
whistled their adequation to a state
        inertly ascertained outside the world
and too well lecturing from their corner box
        as though to measure with a motion there
the wrong idea of reading written in
        the iterationism of the schools
who in idea assisted Jobless there
        to read the letter without opening
ought more of vent than a required cartouche
        could by abrasion worry from the top
powerless alike to think or to repeat
        more than the blazing tapestry on which
his gentle stroked head softly was caressed
        as brave and culpable as plastic best
since no worse insult greets the man of worth
        than to be named an innocent from birth.
Thea had taken the day off.

The Unconditional

        Life is constant and unremitting effort.
           Agramant's GrandAm tagged and manned a rant
of minor speed infractions up until
        the emptiest sierras floated through
a thin disguise of sprawled strip malling where
        a rain of real signals never came
through windshield and his eyeshield on to wet
        receptive surfaces alerted to
the absence of all human hopes and fears.
        Large gulps supped up the infinitely large
or cipher of the infinitely large
        blue marine deserts but in desert shape
like bioluminescent photoforms
        touring abyssal pits in search of food
burn red invisible to blue fish when
        the lit swim turns its scales aside to blur
refrigerated caelocanths may snap
        out from the chiller cabinet with sharp
and legion teeth whose warning is a squint
        or tremor in the lines around the eye
as you stand by the gas pump when they grip
        too hard the nozzle hating every bit
of extra sentience lifting into view
        and then decide to make a meal of you.

The Unconditional

Agramant now depressed his windows by
        a single notch in order better to
breathe in the light gusts of psychosis where
        a possible communication did
after a long refusal now begin
        to form itself to Jobless asking him
to contribute an article to one
        compendium of Agramantine tasks.
Pleasures of Minor Verse still lacked a pen.
        An imperceptible dilation of
the usual block on memory began
        to loosen inside Agramant the ice
permitting all fish skeletons to float
        free in the ether of a fine recall
retrieving piscatory eclogues from
        outlying sculleries of the mansion verse
or Green-land pastorals to sound again
        the finite cupboards of world letters when
a slot comes free for suitors to obtain.
        Hear the whole list of what he shuns to keep
the spleen nailed back inside its bony keep.
        Prove a mere suicide from ease and then
subjocund bottle between six and ten.
        Grazing on ether in the park I choke

The Unconditional

tasting negations one per gulp of smoke.
        A thin tree put a black line on a space
over a concrete fence of abstract place
        requiring even for perception one
archaic effort concentrating some
        resolving love or hatred into thought
flies to those branches from one empty ought
        yet flying not the good but to embrace
the ruined residue of inner space
        or outer futures which till then recede
inside the futureless velocipede.
        Gaunt flora like an eyeball scratch wrote
one bent lash stuck beneath a lid to gall
        expansive motorisms of the road
enough to rip one tear out from that duct
        the driest of all unresponsive flesh
and happening to fall at just that foot
        when with involuntary weakness he
remembering the echo of a dream
        in insubstantial and true contentless
subsynaesthetic wonderings recalled
        one finite doubt of his kind cruelty
enough to let before that raging court
        one single shout of Jobless in his pain

The Unconditional

give to the literal heart one tiny jolt
        producing thus a horrible small slime
of possible truth inside that salty wet
        as though you might find written on his face
more than slow plastics labouring to slip
        one anoriginal indifferent lie
through each dumb doorjamb of the supine world
        when with a small cough Agramant coughed back
forgotten spit which dropping to his lung
        confused his breathing with digestion till
he choked up all loose substances again
        expelled to handkerchief to there sustain
to snotrag there repelled there to sustain
        theodicies of necessary pain.
Now read into those honey-spattered checks
        or monogrammed and snowy linens all
the auguries you ever could demand.
        Where the repulsive gold most thickly flows
or where most sparsely does find its repose
        its thin trails cannot but spell contours which
reweb excreted nets of thinking glitch
        eating away at basiliskal stare
bring on the cruxial imperfection where
        some meaning particle enjoins the next

to blurt out meaning quite outside the text.
        I.e. Agramant was terrified.
One instant of doubt was life in hell.
        Think that those powers you toy with one day can
toy with you hanging from their string or grid.
        Adored psychoses fended off for years
exact their payment not in feeble tears
        but rather just as this repellent mote
stuck in the eyeball scratching out the view
        making the foot limp where it could not see
the right square inch of rubbish to be trod
        calling up rage shot right out to the group
of careless bystanders who give one glance
        at once construed as mockery by who
loses each limb's life in a stumbling drop
        from cruelty to stamped upon from top.
Who are you looking at?
        Who but dispersal of all perilous wish
into the gravy stains on your club tie.
        The personated train processes through
reminding its perennial emptinesses of
        their lost vocations as the agents of
the category superseding each
        wrong good sublation of last year's best thoughts.

Then suddenly the whole tank collapsed in a flood.
        I liked him better when he was a bastard.
It was over as suddenly with a single clench
        of rich dentition in a mended jaw
gripping its no prey to the end of self
        washed in the last time sink and then back out
intersubjectively to sanity.
        Hi suit transparency of frontaging
blurred at its facial edges with a hint
        of stuffed down an experience at the edge
letting the mouth tug scales at corners where
        the razor nicks the skin to rash red star
of emptied willingness to please which on a plane
        of half shaved flesh begs sirs your clemency
once alien to this concentrated beam
        of clever hatreds clearing out the drain.
You're losing it.
        Prove not so now by a swift hit.
Armstrong and Green please by November or
        the 15 quid will go to charity.
That'll sort him.
        =x. can do Somerville.
Just as a small boy one year old may sit
        at poolside looking at his mother's face

The Unconditional

making explicit no one grain of skin
        making no less all knowledge of each thin
line of negation or of affirmation in
        concretely infinite preconnotations which
he knows right now are both the action and
        to one side of the action which you will
test him on later when you want to know
        what he has done today to bring to dust
the glory of the light he first saw when
        I woke and looked out of the window as
I hoped that this time I would be allowed
        not to revert first to the solid spoon
or fork compulsorily intervened
        between him and the colours of the sun.
Just as fresh yellowfin or soft loukoum
        offers a silken innerness to knives
so the white building opened with a gasp
        for Institute of Clinical Phonetics.
Electromyographically $=x$.
        walking on air of earth for one white hour
gulped up a lungful from a fur rubbed plug
        into the abstract tune a single line
traces with finer drips of ink along
        the soundless pathways of phonology

The Unconditional

where the cold syntax of his flushing face
        heating with toneless contrast every beat
suprasegmentally arresting stress
        trod through a pulse with cardiac emphasis.
Two-handed monomorphemes shouted out
        their loudest silent gestures floating doubt
embedding softly with a quiet roar
        the logic of a nameplate into four
preterdissociated skins of sense
        since disciplinary identity
abracadabrawise with one path move
        turns the small sceptic fingerflick into
full throated utterance to me and you.
        Paralinguistic insignificance
in nil insignia mingled in his gin.
        Lump mix of figures rather were the shrill
or hooted feedbacks from the datashell.
        Break my voice into that million,
smithereen palate to immiserates
        working the insect roads across a plane
where no least chitin fragment tinkles in
        no algebraic formulation of no loss
more than a crushed squid bone is known to sing
        nor off a markless pale plateau to ring.

The Unconditional

Resuscitators with aeoliphones
        rush to inject life from the canyons now.
A window gave out on to sweep of hill
        curving with loveliness the sweet grass still
cropped by the many ovine mouths to keep
        its soft hair close against a failing cheek
down to a vale whose curvet to a v
        set J a-tremble out of rising glee
since on the lit slope one small bit of shade
        dropped by a cloud there over that v made
a darker green come over that last spot
        bringing most wildered fancies to this dot
forswearing God the father's fatherhood whereon
        he thought the female tetragrammaton
not as a cut or absent n but then
        full of all brilliant bliss transfigured when
the hills clap hands and oceans do embrace
        shedding their human for one earthly face.
"Look again over this calm mirror.
        Its surface works with nothing every time.
Look at the animation dying for your gaze
        perfectly free from human work or days
slipping with quick meniscus from the grasp
        of all thought smuggled into ought but gasp

then turn that baffled energy against
        anthropomorphitisms and their taints."
Plugged with a finger the fat each man child
        pressed a plump nose up wetly on the glass
wishing to slobber backwards to a past
        nostalgisectors had removed long since
fixed with all blankness into staring green
        with all its power coddled in serene
fields of enquiry sutured by a fence
        marking off orchards for a pear or quince
bearing a limit where his violence
        ripens instead to catch a sight of good
conjecturing indefinitely food
        then with a relaxation by one inch
letting his nose back from the snotted glass
        and eyes drink gently from the window's light
unfallen summer leaves before they turn
        while yet one cooler gust foretells their death
announcing life too in that turning breath.
    3.15. Coffee. Stephen Rodefer Lounge.
All delegates converging from the right
        met with the left ones leaving for the night—
lively controversy viz death warmed up
        squeezes the face from every living thing

The Unconditional

and in whose chilly clubs and lecture halls
        thin subsurrealism rules the field
as nominalist whimsy titters forth
        frog pies exemplify phonology
while blackbird puddings thronging vestibules
        on virtual tables patchily present
the bad non-metaphysics of as if
        then choke on all this merely quoted food
delivered from an instance of the good.
        I am your mother coming back in light.
I am your father in this pure new white.
        Turn back again now to those powerless
and bankrupt elements whose slaves
        you want to be all over again--
while J's at last achieved no irony
        fixed no expression on his face but see
what would turn up in hour from three to four
        a radical empiricist at last
willing to let all things fall through the box
        solidifying from his melting flux
or scree of secondary qualities
        into all proper singularity
and taste of their own unheard and true name
        first from the trap in form of a lapel

The Unconditional

clair or obscur affiliated well
        and where black serifs mirrored with their fit
the too stretched corners of a cracking smile
        his patron Agramant shoving a clumsy fist
out as a handshake into his unkissed
        gut or chest area which just too late
J went to hold inside his own wet palm
        making the smile turn down its corners in
a frown of disapproval for slight pain
        and hand rip backwards from botched greeting to
motion across to plains of seatage which
        offered their plywood acres with a yawn
to modern personages sitting down
        sinking with slight report into the foam
sheathed in a viscose blanket all of beige.
        "Coffee?" "No thanks." These two words like small stones
dropped a new sound into A's ear and head.
        In some impoverished province of that state
a government inspector had been shot.
        The household cavalry in mid wheel flinched
sticking to orders feeling one wrong note
        proceeding none the less to dogmatize
well varying their one unshining theme
        Pleasures of Minor Verse which made to teem

The Unconditional

expound all protocols expelling thought
        from each last paragraph which talks of ought
and rudely broken by impatient glance
        from Jobless out to rectangle of light
determining his foe and patron there
        to close the contract with what force majeur
his beating brow could muster with its hair
        knotted emphatical in scansion graph
cut off in mid pitch by a flat "OK"
        behind which his near gasp almost discerned
a little pinhole vision of that scope
        of unconditional truth de minimis
twitching its thinking muscle up to top
        (so in a line of Dyer's *Fleece* you read
all the eternity you'll ever need)
        and meekly uttering for all return
just "Good. That's good" and flopping weakly back
        in a flat sea of plastic butterscotch.
His client's face seemed newly organized
        bearing the pressure of precise intent
shining with no psychosis but a thought
        and an eye focussed on no point but that
held immaterially to light from out
        the luminating unreflected beams

The Unconditional

darkening with concentration at the brink
        of each live eye or mouth hole membrane couched
yet holding secret all its inner sense
        a fine one particle within him sings
doing what A's fat textbook says you can't
        willing a meaning to the edge of birth
renewing thought in beating down all dearth
        as when apparently from scraps of noise
apparently not placed but simply thrown
        or simply falling through the atmosphere
a non contingent pressure or a sense
        patterns a ripple or a pulse of skin
or reaches with a tongue tip to announce
        both what it wants to taste and what it speaks
or trips along a lawful palate so
        as magic floating down to earth or so
ascending to no other place than this
        circumference of objects thinking bliss
or central bosom of all mutual aid
        infinitesimally melody
willed and invented or retrieved and made
        consuming air, creating for a song
law free from an exception or a verse
        as in a sole just flood which only bursts

The Unconditional

the wrong abstraction leaving else upright
        a sister string tense only to a sound
or one free face of equal good alive
        with luck without stupidity at last
Leonora
        which Agramant could only gaze and scan
as threat lines forming from unthinking man
        reading both right and wrong that furrowed Y
made by the tightening of nose to eye
        as J just watched repayment creases form
on Agramant's whole hating map of scorn.
        "I forgot milk." None is to be found here.
The half cloud half and cuckoo land elsewhere
        leaves spectral cartons as its shadow here
which Agramant shuffling across to fetch
        give J his exit to get up and walk
across the room working itself with talk
        out up the hill and on in consciousness
of each loose stone speaking beneath his feet.
        While Agramant does hardly dare return
but with a shift of non fat milk hunt skulks
        off to his room and lock the door to slump
there in a quarter effortfully soothed
        with a long list of all J's errors made

The Unconditional

beginning with Idealism and
        ending with failing to repay fifty quid.
The king bed propped a lozenge in the tight
        and orangeish expanses of the suite
follow its central whopper with a light
        fringed with restraining tassels as off beat
alternate green and orange cushions sat
        blankly spectating over yards of pile
the pink pale orange carpeting or fat
        pupplastic memory of wool could smile
while in the bottom left the sparkling wine
        piped celebration from its bulbous top
chilled in the bucket for a special time
        perking its end out over a blue drop
which the flat window opened out before
        in monochrome of winding sheet sky blue
neatly bisected aluminiumwise by poor
        glazing dividers carving up a view
shedding no light into the low rich room
        not at once lost inside its umber glade
dying the instant that it met that gloom
        darker than visible or human shade.
The failing narcopops in mezzotint
        revenged faux pacifyings with their skint

outorted engineries of deject
        moralized emblems printed in select
serries of death's-heads gawping from the top
        singing a little pic to cheer him up
7 beasts poking heads out from a globe
        with a small cross on top conceal the leg
of Woodtop Sapiens who stands behind
        a hen's head hiding his devoided groin
with one arm out flat next as though to show
        all the world's miseries have got to go
while in his right a global apple sits
        scarcely more tempting than those thickened fits
of dire calamities which burble on
        in the themed weather all back toys put on
as wind-head, tost-ship, lightning-fork and Fire
        offer abstract rebuke to all desire
while in the foreground the schematic grass
        writes similies for flesh in shorthand's last.
Apparition of the Eternal Church!
        How in scenery of some grey or other proposed set
Sky which already in its refusal of monotone
        Greyly or otherwise appears given over to withheld
Signification in the surmised grip of an author or printer'
        S mark scratched out for example on the idea of a for example in clouds

S to all eye written in a matter of freezing water about to become rain
        Shifting whose small and scarce moving part of a weather front
Apparently animates what cannot be construed as a face yet cannot be
        Construed as not a face either since it is like that a surface which works
Or with meaning plays like a sea or like another such surface which can
        Be a term of comparison or which can not be if you wish
Free to fail
        So would the firmament of course appear in an idea of charactery at that
Instant when a scene of lament is prepared for a free floating
        Pineapple or other sheer token perfectly freed of all nature or knowing
Nature is itself essentially some squid bone or other graphic substrate or dust
        Set to return to scratch or eat dirt or to inaugurate with a
Zero the self-sabotaging or self-salvaging calculus of squid parts burnt
        To thin washes or their cross-hatch effigies or other bone leavings of what
Makes an appropriate hole off of which or out of which the proper ray
        Or proper series of divergent light ink diagonals can sing or can be a sign
Or something
        Floats up as if to say
Please in any case welcome
        Perfect terror and anagnorisis of the Church scored by a pupil of Dukas and Dupré
As for early horror silents and with some of the same lighting
        So please in case from your hell home
Know your cell preknown by this quite terrifying assembly or spaceship
        Or please then fold or please do not then drone

Or do not more than with an array of tongue clicks meant for prayer fall down
    Utterly abashed
Until the bell sounds
    And switch off.
When it to a false point like the dot in television recedes I can see the numerous stars
    Scattered in different directions sweep all alike across the sky every day continuously for ever
Doubly both endless plural and otherwise police or haul a circuit of alloy and allude
    Doubly both and nor otherwise circling to a retained identity as of inhuman aluminium
Or can see how however the axis does not move even slightly from its place but stays
    I like an atalantine or look like a talon landed or a tank rotating
The sky itself incautiously spent
    Depleted like purples
And then stoked up with acorn replacements or vapour trails
    Whose signatures may be iterated in the attempt to nominate
Perfection in convergence which however remaining asymptotic can fail for good
    To arrive at more than a styled lyrical stroke of waste or just feeling across the optical blue.
To arrive at more than their stroke, a waste of just feeling across the optical blue.
    To arrive as more than a vapour a melange or s-me devoured melisma pours melodious blue
So as no more than a devout reproof veers a line of exhaust gas in its course of blue
    So as not to do more than provide an improved curve an analysis insists that the sky is not blue
But backlit or construed rather summoning a pure spectral presence as if you
    Or as if all this were real
Which for a second it is
    So when I say

Anything like it
>Listen to the bass of get stupid fresh part two

Whatever
>Or to whatever variable may be the condition of your ceasing to discount your experience

And named thus indefinitely not just for bathtime in Sardis
>But rather because a proper name is precisely not meaningless nor precisely

Meaningless in many different ways but instead
>Precisely in the way of what might properly be named as meaning

May so much more instantly at an occasion prompt the descent of a stomach floor
>Or may so much more durably over an epoch glint as a target for

Whatever may definitely be wished for as a star outline of visible signs
>Near which circles a shape like a man working

Just called on his knees.
>Out from the sounding mountains all alone

She towards evening would emerge and walk
>Not engaging anyone in friendly conversation.

Light from a depressed angle swept far across the lake.
>Small craft could over an expanse of water be seen

Plying in apparently perfect contingency
>Lines whose written total may not be summed or read

For just which purpose the pilots at leisure determined
>Long courses from port to port as though intoning under the breath a relieving

Interval or an interposition or an episode in an incomplete long narrative whose charm
>Shades interstitially its chief pleasure in a cool or sheltered transition or subplot

Disowning its own crimes as the necessary condition of their own final effacement
        Into a certain grey that uncertainly is lit with a concealed sun
Just as the word ordinary is uncertainly lit with the promise of extra which is both
        Bracketed and held or suspended and possessed by its irrealizable adventure of pure disposition
In which I settle for as the tepid element or medium of a life some supposed demos
        In the event
  Murderous scorching imperium
        When she from off the earth
Just flew with a frown and shrug
        To where she is still invisible
But still made visible
        Not as a norm or value but a star
Series by night as if a maiden near to polyskeptical Arctophylax
        Shining over a non astral plane we scour
Hoping that quantity to quality
        Turn at a holy nail for ever free
Or stellify in luminous desire
        What can alone with real loss be understood as alone the value of a bound variable.
Long televisual etceteras lulled
        with unaccustomed flickerings his spleen
or other organs bleating of new fear
        where the republican lurched bottlewards
scarcely discerning gilt crests on its glass
        impounded by appointment to the crown

The Unconditional

nor of no relevance when gulping down
        slugs of right royal vodka by the gill
tending those wounds would rather die than spill
        out to the general he hourly serves
while the police spoils all the best tunes still
        (It is more difficult to save than kill.
Nakedly the old Adam gets up.
        It a gulping flesh grips up in the throat.
Bliss was like just all over the place.
        I think up Jill and Bob in a slick kiss.
Bill comes back blubbing from the garden shed.
        Jill thinks Bob back from the dead in a
jobless bliss up or a bawling lack.
        I thought off Bill and Jo in a picked fist.
Bob weeps back rubbing down a concrete bed.
        Jo brings Bill back from the shed in a
paid so sad down off of a full pack.
        Da capo until the stick wears down.
Endure thus much fun and escape alone
        to tell the indifferent world of what you did.
In sad perplexity of false delights
        I would place now a heart and now a star
upon the breathing frame of beauty where
        I love the portrait of my future end

The Unconditional

pleading for shelter and a kind of cool
        interposition shading in a cloud
as all the art you'll ever need floats down
        from inexhaustible arrays of light
nailed to a twitch or impulse of my thumb
        or adding textage from reverted love
hour after hour I stare past what you are.
        A wet lip crawled up and its labour drew
respite from inanition creeping through
        her arteries which diving from the air
scurried from scent or atomies that were
        when through my eyes the pixellated east
too torpid divagated from its feast
        of these crumbs while a distant noise of mirth
or sansjoy shifted accidental earth
        conducting one fear of a loss that might
ruin all present pleasure or delight
        that eats into a seed or mask of man
since the first life in the first world began
        to waste or tickle through a limb or vein
and loves and hatreds with their clicks or pains
        to leak a damp in insulating felt
or heat up fixtures to a shapeless melt
        beyond the power of the ageing sun

The Unconditional

whose few cloud fragments only are undone
        by nothing of his work but melt away
in rosy ruin and yellow spoil of day
        or burn a name down to its sponsored sense
clear of typography or more incense
        with light from inward and with effluent heat
a thing like pleasure through our hands and feet.
        And as a future suicide to dawn
tends to an image of the love withdrawn
        or as a photograph of girls afloat
on piles of rubbish which a masher smote
        yet could not quite destroy within an hour
so on a tarmacadam surface flower
        scraps of metallic red before they broke
rose-fashion upwards to the gazing stroke
        or down to shatter on the path there came
both skin and bone in refuge from a flame:
        translating Mayday to a flight or swoon
always already blasted before June.
        So towards space a heart and thorax burned.
Then the discarded fuel stages turned
        and fell to ocean while her new mouth smiled
as though the spirit and sense unreconciled
        shrank too indifferently from the hour

when life dies to a revocable flower.
        The carpal muscles work right up and down
in writing or in wasting book or creed
        as glum jig lumping jambs of foot to knee
working a threadbare patch of carpet where
        perfect aggression leaks into my hair
hating until four thousand and then stop
        sleeping eyes open till the lid must drop
stoking an obsolescent engine or
        pumping the blood with poison primers for
black circulations hollow echoing
        the real economy of real things
immeasurably distant planets spend
        wasting their gases to no useful end
the note of warmest feeling supplements
        in darkened parlours waiting on events.
Sad Strains Of Gay Waltz By B. Gael Zeblub.
        "How do they know which dark heart to invade?
How does a thief know where the silver lies
        but by some grains of sand he sows into
the empty chamber hoping for a light
        infinitesimally audible
mere ringing with direction to his paw
        as pealing back suggestions from a fort

The Unconditional

too well defended from a happy thought
        bells of all evil distantly recount
willing accomplices' apprentices.
        That melody of sand is what I hear
in every conversation nowadays.
        In Nowadays, by X melodious sand
I hear the atrophy of any hand
        coloraturously as it once leapt
an ought from cold Kamschatka to Cape Horn
        the furnace of humiliation now
is a light suntan on a face that wept
        some traffic problems outside Old Gwangchow.
How could they not see that the verb to be
        was from my novel carefully left out?
No doubt I should have advertised the fact
        then to be styled an impresario
or wizard both of freedom and constraint."
        "As I don't miss it in your sort of life
I then don't miss it in your book as well.
        What you hack off it with your paper knife
receives its proper value in a hell
        of Chinese cities made up for the rhyme
pre-polished to deletion of what time
        nil admirari mirrors back to those

The Unconditional

staring too long into their own repose."
        Pips lisp or piss to slip you lippery blisses
then write down each of his inexpert kisses
        em purple or they pink to royal snails
as unobtainable in these locales
        and therefore best for kings to tread upon
with every frisson that can thus assure
        by guilt or pain that some large principle
is served by any single grain of muck
        that leaves the boot to dwell in tapestry
as wandering thexpensive groves emong
        some coldest campery proposes love
as the bare echo of its former joys
        (some some, some summary or surmise) floats
to find no sumptuary terminal
        but diligent with lostness to defer
those mortal fabrics never known to err:
        Tertullian saintlessly remaindering
unsainted Origen remouldering
        or Valentinian retraitoring
unsaint-traditionally rendering
        the heavenly cobalt upwards to its true
unheavenly parablisses of the few
        immoderate joys that yet remain to sing

or parapurple remnants lyricking
>	the new returning bliss percussively
the infanitesimal lips regressively
>	mimickerist delight concussively
the new cerulean excessively
>	the superspectral white depressively
the unendurable light recessively
>	the unreturning earth untentedly
the inaccessible dearth contentedly
>	the communist heaven intoxicate
the communist earth rededicate
>	the communist word reuninterpret
the communist life inexcavate
>	the communist shoe unwearable
the communist true unbearable
>	the communist food uneatable
 the communist wish untreatable
>	the communist green invisible
the communist red-red-risible
>	the communist love immedicable
the communist sex unimaginable
>	the communist hymn unsingable
the communist thing intangible
>	the communist unprefungible

is communist art unfundable:
        grin; squirt; cough; mutter; grimace; titter; boo
and other pert devices deafen you
        while auras of the impermeable shield
return all bad intentions to the place
        a sealed cosmology prepares for them
and for us also in our interior hearts.
        Published from Nauvoo at the Only Press:
An Odal Fragment from the Reformed Egyptian
        or last cotillion of the Anti-Bank
for Polly Sweat, Elizabeth McFate
        ("I only lived because I could not die")
and several members of the Sick Detachment.
        "The Anti-Bank burns money to keep warm.
Beneath preserving smoke we store the dead
        waiting to rebaptize them properly
into the wonder of these later days
        where apostolically luminous
accords proclaim the obvious fallacy
        that any life whatever be here now
and earn the hatred of the waning world
        which hugs its comfortable deathmask on.
Decline all growth. Refuse to sign as wealth.
        Dollars of Anti-Bank believe and try

The Unconditional

to mint negation as a part of sky.
        Perplexed among the sandbars Mendelssohn
would reach you from the distant camp of saints
        inducing others to devise a plan
to bury a piano in the dirt
        against that time when all shall rise again
or by six muddy feet at least go up
        to perfect Zion, broken down for scrap."
Combusted gasoline yelled to redrench
        suchsung archaic liars in grosser notes
but ever under it the awkward hymn
        plodded defatigably to its capital.
Aegyptian strain which other voices joined.
        "The more we echo to our living skins
("as matter thinks its thoughts in the object through
        or as the dull true testimony moves
to weeping those who hear and know it true")
        the more material song becomes our skins.
The more their perfectless transcendence yells,
        the more their emptiless interiors ex-
(so nothing laboriously ex-deject)
        dejected traverse on a contour map.
While we hymn hagio-gazetteers of place
        their bone directories leave any where

The Unconditional

obscenest stuff excrete from spirit-gods.
          We gather that and nurse it back to life
knowing this so-spoke junk not quite bereft
          of absolute vestige is the absolute itself.
These mudmarks are the last good mudmarks left
          of any handcart's writing on the earth.
These latifundia of agricult
          cover a spot where memorable pain
endured and leaves its absolute fact in earth.
          Although a cool mind sets these traces by,
the earth might think itself no other now;
          its irrevocably transacted face
lies as though listeningly under all language."
          This on a silical deleterbase
deeply deleted in the temple vault.
          Deeply now gas-yells cover it with ought.
Its thrice-reproved willed nullity was tagged
          with this curt criticism's number-seal:
"You hymn Ur-earthish from a dataport.
          With each net loss you print up as a gain
one quantum thinner bangs the autogong.
          You only taste the life you say you are.
This or that content fills up any jar."
          A slow cold settles on the perfect dead.

None knows if ought retrieve them from that shed.
        Then on reflection added these remarks:
"No wonder that the prophet let himself
        in revelation take so many wives.
His whole delirium is the identical lurch
        to when a sensed and infinitesimal twitch
of any desiring finger in the public
        street or in the office maybe turns
the inside out to what its darker shade
        knows as the public claim of private lust:
the inner twitch it blusters into life
        takes its sad motion from the languaged masks
it writes off as the doubtable coverings
        (or legal dead walking the ocean floor)
jurassic markets of the mask-folk made:
        while all the while this thinking-thinking gland
ingests all nutriments from the self same sump
        it then voids on our heads as "ideology".
The continuity of revelation bears
        the same bad standards as our later ills
which Totally for blood and earth came out
        and with those proto-publics personed it."
Then criticism fixed itself a slug
        of gin and vermouth from a nearby fridge.

The Unconditional

Cold spirits waited there in readiness
        where lights and colours of a brilliancy
matched only by the grey in grey of prose
        sprang on the wondering eye when opened up
greens puces purples faintly glistening
        to it the bracketed then more sweet reward
of any self confessed complicity
        (I love the animals by eating up)
which still negates the fluids it consumes,
        still in a No retains its airy room
still in its good No shelters colours where
        effortless polychromes perplastic their
greyest bright pinks and oranges as
        harshly attack the eye from any shirt
or jocose jacket wandering down the street.
        Without that No a Yes Yes dawdles out
privated fun as though for public good.
        La Celestina elanguescently
bespeaks the part death plays in happiness.
        She speaks it too with ungainsayables.
Around her where the impossible tigers lounged
        brute Tamerlane gave out that reedy note
whose tone sunk empires of the east in song
        (the deities from the western seaboards there

The Unconditional

all cloudiestly could and did assume
        their tiptop allegory in gossamer
personing each a minute particular
        aut factical aut magical and so
most properly sequestered in their baths).
        'Around' because his precise location was
quite indiscernible in the orient fog
        of the historicizing slideshows' gorgeous blur:
Material specificity divine!
        Largely revealing and reveiling you
to positively magical effect
        desublimatingly inertly stellify
a matt-gloss shine-concretion I slip off
        into the outer darkness of the concept!
M-Specificity disluminable!
        Your grove not to be enlightened where the dark
gleam falls thickly on whatever is described
        then smuggles the punished agalmata through
craqueluriest guilt-imputations:
        so nodding horrors brownly overhang
the lit cot alchemizing them to some
        surmised recuperated prodigal
excess of too familiar happiness:
        where patterned plates shall index with each coy

so bloody shepherdess the national debt
        ("These joys are too abundant to be real.")
Snigger at "Lady Cockburn with her babes"
        ditto "proud paterfamilias on his knees"
as thence dead end of dead lit. politics
        weak no-amusement from ten podia drips
culling what tiniest tremor of what thrill
        from Emily Potts as Thaïs setting fire
to old Persepolis in effigy)
        art after art goes out to grass and then
draws a long draft of crystal from the bank
        where purlingly the contextualized gore slips by.
That slideshow is the pastoral it condemns.
        The rural notes it cannot ever hear
still in a pasture better bleat the end
        of what would wish still to erase them quite
than all the regiment of brightly clad
        smartish expositors of destiny.
Because their comfortlessness warmly wraps
        them in a lethal warm car or fat plane
they must not hear that shepherds still exist,
        much less hear how to shelter from the rain.
Laziness and love both must die out again.
        Affirmative modernism art-side gives to these

The Unconditional

the pleasures of negation minus guilt
        braying in acid lime eleetists down
free from nostalgia as from any pain
        or from complicity with any ill:
free then from any possibility
        of bad returning to a "mythical":
free from bad wishes for totality:
        free from bad longing for a mother's breast.
Affirmatively willing to perform
        all tasks asked of it in the classrooms where
Affirmatively willing to affirm
        essence of affirmation in its blanc
then just add content to the crunchy tank.
        Taste of destruction made that bliss complete
until another day should break the pane
        or old life shit its excrements again.
The poordunk scareheads scattered to decay.
        Yet to this no reply proceeded not
from all negated mouths that stood around
        as catachretic as they well could be
agape with disbelief at what was said
        of their own nullity when all the time
they felt to know themselves to know and feel
        as sentient as the next real uttering star.

The Unconditional

So taciturnly this unspoken word:
      "Slow coaches crawl into the glimmering west.
We crawl too slowly our unshimmering best.
      However many hatreds fall upon
our necks we always get there in the end."
      A railway in its obsolescent course
returns to Omsk its worst, to Tomsk its harms;
      a road pantravellably dashes all
into the pansecured retrashed alarms;
      a service station in the desert cures
more than a monkish breakdown in the cell;
      stations of pain which ever set their lures
just where the credulous could want to tell;
      there all the demons convocating best
found a new sin exquisitely repressed;
      there in the pectoral of judgement dressed
was a gay fitness murderously expressed;
      that morning as we came over the Scete
a light which slanted from the eastern sky
      could unconceal the dwellings in the rock
which incavated it on every side
      and all reminded us of harbours where
a refuge from the impending disaster was
      still less a refuge than the improbable place

where in its apparent abstractness a thought
>	or feeling or thought-feeling sometime might
against the all-imminent surrender live
>	or where say rather the eternal truth
theme this but little heard of among flies
>	could in the demise of all intention plan.
At False Parting of the Ways I sank.
>	We bear our shades about us; self-deprived.
"How can a critical intellectual use
>	the very terms that she at once
subjects to a searching criticism?"
>	The same way I fall asleep when you talk.
How can a bad thought wither, fail and die?
>	By the same power that the sun goes out.
In almost total hatred soothe a self
>	with nightly reading of the catechists.
"There is no sexual relationship."
>	"It was Barred S who did it and since he
is only present in his absence I
>	advise you drop the charges officer."
Who, to one side, is that?
>	*His path in scrub diminishes itself.*
Behind him do
>	*the branches shut up tight again to close.*

The Unconditional

The grass stand up again.
*   Who now may ease those pains when any balm*
turns for him poison soon ever as touched?
*   First was despised and so he now*
turned best despiser eating up his cash
        insatiably consumes all innerness.
Labours of love exhaustingly destroyed
        as patiently as endeavouring parasites build;
labours of love worked to a careful void
        by every succour less preserved than killed;
electing fixity electively to inter
        the indelibly chosen character of love
choosing the burial of please defer
        all colour to all other there above;
the coldest and the meanest of all lives
        chops up its vegetables with meaning there;
the supplement of sold work never gives
        ought but a repetition of that air:
Big other weeping in the shrubbery
        while D stares fixedly into a drink
so face to face and wound to wound they join
        in a twinned labour which the walls unthink.
O in Your repertoire of human tones
        if there exist perceptible to ears

The Unconditional

some quiet note with power to dissolve
        the preknown objects which the tough brain hears,
refresh this breathing relic at the bone
        or thus by lonely dissonance unresolve
all the wrong solid harmony of fears!
        Refresh this heart with new deserts.
Contactless eye, why do you wander away?
        Cold credit-face, where munch up your shame?
Contactless eye, to which too fixive horizon
        where Creditface do you weep the hoarded tears?
You are the true trustless planet hovering
        into the uninhabitably grey
indifferentiated enterpot
        or impossibly elisory era I would think
had never a could a been in any age:
        Just as it is in truth impossible
to walk indifferently past whoever knows
        your face and therefore if they do not seem
to see you this is well named cutting you.
        So a yellow throat whitens to its old tutor.
There is no neutrality lived on earth.
        I look another human in the eye.
What do I see there but the world's mid-night
        negating possible transparency

of recognitions in its infinite
        opaque or loveless necessary thing
"he refused to make eye contact with me."
        "Yes risible checkout monster I subsist
Yes at the secular instant I decline
        Press Yes press No press Press-depressive press
"I am not able to be able" so
        I live in the gap between the belt and exit.
Cards, cash and salad fragments get to me
        mishidden in a comfortable nest
where the impertinent gaze may never come.
        The large states guarantee obscurity.
The queerest symbolist in the whole bank.
        You can got to sleep in that uh dark den all.
Believe it that this breath-exstriction can
        alone of suffocations now extant
still imprecipitate precipitate
        the one true good and beautiful
bent neck for the coming anthology:
        the absolute dejection which you say
is unausdenkbar I quite contrary
        breathe as the daily pseudo-food there is
Then pseudoexcrement is the downshot!
        Lacking the alone reality of dung

scarfing my gullet up to the top pitch
        where almost fatal thinness of the air
ecstatically near unbreathing which
        tops off a mopped mouth with a stopper where
no call of horns may sound so sweet nor sour
        dimly resounding through the summer trees
nor can chromatically circling keys
        torqued in orchestral enginery of bliss
accelerating crabwise through all our
        possible stops of numbered feeling at
all come all open like the minute when   [Agramant (*sarcastically*):
        I just break up and then to other lips   *Isolde!*
this hell of immanence at last goes down   *Tristan!*]
        and I precisely can say that I then
not as beneath this arch proscenium lies
        the starry sky of any rentier
imprisoned infinite in living-room
        but rather with my still believing flesh
down to the letter of my spirit do
        love at the moment when I must die twice."
"Then invade Poland shortly afterwards.
        My serious advice is that you read with care
the papers for tomorrow's meeting first.
        Then get drunk at the weekend if you must.

The Unconditional

I don't care for Flagstad's 1953 myself.
        Sousa's your man for all that sort of stuff."
A spaceship sailed away into the deep
        lulled by the love duet from *Alien Film*.
A notch more cruelty was cut into
        the marked assessments of the spirit-drudge.
Erotic longing longing to decree
        marched out the door and slammed it longingly.
How much is everything? What else is there?
        The conference of 1956
stared with a snowblind discipline across
        its philological Antarctica.
Exhilarating candours lay ahead.
        Outposts, crevasses, blubber, motorsleds.
Harsh winters in the iron libraries
        packing the fire into an inner glow
barely detectible to any glance
        tamped down beneath a cloth exterior.
Those icecaps melt and rapidly recede.
        Of all art's science scarce a steely frown
tugs at a facial muscle not prewarmed
        by too conversant smoothing novelty.
Accessibility spills stickily
        into a friendly vacuum or a sump

subversively to blur the boundaries
>	=dead and alive out-inside pastel glop.
I stroke *The Calculus of Variants*
>	nearly beside myself with pained return
at how much loyalty to the Idea
>	is woven there into the diagrams
believing these to be the carapace
>	whose damageable adamantine shrinks
likely to die at any human touch
>	and therefore sealed implacably below
the black stemmata of an age quite lost
>	precluding triage of the varia
with binding under every former joy
>	to bury passion for an inky god
while yet the paper is a feather bed
>	or softest undergarment for the sense
swaddled in cream and curds between the boards
>	till rightly deaccessioned by the group
of meaning letterists at serverbase
>	folding a presence into every bite
and inescapably refeeding all
>	to lick the plate of words clean till we chuck
from bloated empty stomachs in again
>	stuffed fit to burst with slimming agents where

The Unconditional

in every cell of pan-publicity
        perpetual celebration sadly tells
an inverse Eucharist in clicks and bells.
        Mass in a vindicated sector please.
All which impels this poem to set down
        no-methodologies to editors
or mere chaimeras of the poet's brain
        gathered from all no-readers up again.
Just as the sunlight on a microscreen
        makes all illegible the writing there
so may my worst words be forgotten quite
        leaving no more trace than the air in air.
Nothing is happening to me yet again.
        O wrenches, tremblings, dizzinesses, spells!
Mises-en-abîme of the most terrible kind!
        O pure bedazzlement of the singular!
And all in this office on the thirteenth floor!
        Presuicidal chocolatiers
coat morsels with a delicate agony
        for which their German reading long ago
was the how cost effective entrance fee
        ("In every line that Celan ever wrote
hovers a brooding ethical concern":
        poor penny dreadfuls of the critical scene

where the quotidian shopping carts unseen
> gather to give this hulking strut the lie

full of their viands for the evening pie.
> The worst that is thought and known in the world.

Precisely instead unriddable pleasures
> the poet gripped until he fathomed them wet.

(How precisely the joyful idiot is snubbed
> the courtiers of singularity

can well arpeggiate as they now tread
> on underlings of idiotism who

know little of the sacrifices made
> by the sole selfers walking on their guts.

(Tsk my ressentimentful prosodist!
> Excellent rancour from the hilltop sire!

When may we know what you yourself have lost
> or ever had to put up in the rain?)))

paid on the dot in job talks now and then.
> "Whither then art and its relation to virtue?

The answer unfortunately is nothing at all.
> Just take the famous occasion on which

the camp guards wept at Schubert as they worked."
> Whilst these extremely valuable thoughts

were syndicated over the mute earth
> a symphilosophist at once composed

The Unconditional

(nudged by some measures of D. 959
        drifting across the kitchen into him)
inelegant retorts despite himself:
        "Historia sacra of your outer death!
How many a want supplies that dismal scene!
        Raison d'état of the alibi subrepublic!
You fantasize yourself a party guest
        at the so yearned for olde Totentanz.
How eagerly you love to make the worst
        your paradeigma of the attainable real
or cut off all the bloody bits that do not fit
        to make a sacrifice of any wish.
Without that tale your self-revolted ear
        would be compelled to listen to the notes
and entertain the possibility
        (so well reviled beyond all other ill)
that finitely they mean and obligate
        the unlucky listener to some real path.
Anyone can listen to Schubert stupidly.
        That no more tells us what the music means
than your dumb op-ed column can endure
        the quiestest element of a human wish.
Comb then the lives of all bad anti-saints
        for all unholy relics of that hour

The Unconditional

when you were exculpated from all good
        and with it any need to make one shift
in the long easy chair of culture chat.
        O rather may those storied tears become
a flood willing to bear all cruelty off
        into an ocean deep enough to sink
the worst forever in oblivion where
        it meets its water-grave eternally
than have their salty pipes and tubings stopped
        by any pan-self-immolating smirk
secretly hoping for the very end."
        But fellow critics shuffled in their seats.
"All, each, and every, are the words you choose.
        Pop-panlogistic in the simplest sense
don't you drown out an audible rustle
        whose quiet scepticism undersings
the pomp topped bombast of your charmless trump?
        Think about it." The darkening metro droned
a low yes yes to each and all of them.
        Suddenly ascending sounds of sliding doors
sang through the front of the head in pure joy
        which two whales spouting on the beach could hear
as a precise equivalent of the raven dance
        —as unpreowned as indominionable—

The Unconditional

emptying the house of all fog surfaces
        supplied from Hudson Bay or anywhere else.
Keen in the bitter wind like infinite grief.
        "He wants to eat the whole world for himself.
Or want to eat it up but could not reach.
        With both hands he eats at the edge of the world
then vomits for all the inverse satisfactions."
        Refreshing vertigos of turning down
the stocks who tumble where they choose to go
        like beingless becoming darkening
and melting into inexistent air
        or ever in the noplace foundering
against their own renihilable tide
        changeless decay eternally unlives
silver as unsubstantial futures fly
        swift in their joy but swifter in despair
resolving agony to metaphor
        as figures there are all the loss I know
plummeting dumbly in the intense inane.
        Get me a quote on debris and body parts.
Ignore the inconvenience of being dead.
        They love their Transzendenzzusammenhang
the more in every feature it irreals.
        "When I may speak of swoons and tremblings

know that these are not such in the sense
        that any one might see us ontically
falter or drop, no! the very reverse.
        These words are meant transcendentally.
To understand this see reverse of packet.")
        just as the sky goes further off and grows
less like the air one soul can breathe or know.
        Every little thing's going to be all right.
So says the bottom of the glass in spades.
        A glazing over yet to drone of screen
sees in an acreage of sponsored baize
        Satan at matchplay bowls give him one grin
coming as though straight out of the machine
        inviting Agramant to notice well
how all made things wag gently round to hell.
        Strong Poets flopped around beside the pool
grimacing as the Weaker brought them drinks
        (whose think-transporters would shed half their load
for one smile from the lips of Frank Kermode)
        thus interrupting the important work
of strenuous clinamens sightlessly
        performed by leaving out what most they loved
while turning deaf ears to all mere technique
        preferring Theoria to the sleek

> How is it then, being both the best general and the best rhapsode among us, that you continually go about Greece rhapsodizing and never lead our armies?

or roughened particles of letterage
        (Strong Poets rather in their tax returns
Strong than in spoken numbers or what yearns
        for fluid artifice as knowledge when
the lumpen maestro cannot count to ten
        (resentful mastix o' resentment why
I bite back weakly from my toothless eye
        (or rather float up with a careless joke
than take your breath away with violent smoke
        puffed from the family romance of Grubb
longing to fly but still condemned to blub)))
        sifting their irritations deep within.
Grit to no oyster of their no pearl din.
        Even these mirror-circuits half looked up
when a bright light flared somewhere in the sky.
        Qnuxmuxkyl screwed his tense clear retina
into eve's one dim sharpened dusk
        watching a single comet pass and die
shedding sidereal no-influence
        save for one lucky blinding mote which falls
right in the pupils of renowned Pierre Bell
        to furnish critic magnifying glass
but seen by Q with fine indifference
        spent effortlessly on the sky yet still

earnt by long years of disenchanted skill
        idly all working up to perfect cold
stilled in the indigo of real reserve.
        Qnuxmuxkyl drew another gulp of dross
passing it through opposing currents which
        measured that fat gas on his metal lungs
against the only ether fit to breathe
        captured in Davos 1921
rated the higher for small oxygen
        inducing special efforts of the chest
to draw thin fluids from surrounding skies
        diffracting all the breathable events
ever arriving at his cloudy tent.
        The blue deep darkened; the declining west
foundered beneath the cars in golden vest
        just as a slight chill brushed the sleeping wave
of Q's loose skin too dormant to repave
        his thin distinguished upper arm with hair
standing up stiff from off the cold skin there
        sending a shiver to the waiting brain
recruited instantly to thought of pain
        surmised to power cosmos both and skin
concentering all history within
        the fateful bristling of his chilly arm

The Unconditional

blest with some intimation of new harm.
        Why are the stars so hard to see and read?
Were equal brilliance allied to fire
        leaving no defect in the line of light
but visibly refiguring in flame
        each schema floated by the selfish name
incendiary suffering would shake
        this frame of signals from its earthly make.
The sky would burn down to its carbon last
        or sea dry out in heat of colourfast
too mobile purples searing to its bed
        all motherless matter with its sleepy head.
Junk king it then or would with a sung click.
        Star to star answers. As a beacon line
brings information at the speed of light
        a starry outline designates a shape
sufficiently illuminating fate.
        The comet tailed out from its final swerves.
Nothing had happened. The resisting trees
        stood woodenly around the grey green park
refusing to predict their future leaves'
        shapes or existence in the gathering dark.
The not innumerable potential flowers
        had no thought whether in that tended place

stalk might push blossom up a little space
        to colour any line with real powers.
There in the distance Q saw =x. and J
        stroll with their slowest tread across the field
proclaiming thoughtful leisure at each pace
        with hyperbolic languour so becalmed
that Q began to doubt each time
        the heavy foot went up that it could fall
(That conversation lacks a record now.
        The sole left monument of all that age
lives in the sketch one essay precomposed
        by one participant who travelled back
by rail while scribbling in a little book.
        J at that moment as the sheep rolled by
helplessly static in the slaughterfields
        reverted with renewed love to the thought
of how with exoteric scale his essay might
        meet all criteria syndics could lay down
yet also with its inside meaning hum
        an undersong of proper disrespect
proposing by adjustment of the pause
        a general theory of idolatry
which not alone insiders might decode
        but rather the far smaller group who read

The Unconditional

one line and then the next and so as far
        as sense could bear a meaning up and out
sensing in tremors of the beaten line
        no advance warning of the credit net
more than one breath upon an open face
        tells to the dilettante craving face
sending a weak glance up to the rock face
        wishing to visit every blurred no place
neither hyletic nor noetic in
        nor stuffs nor thinking swimming or within
a dry wet is ought station in no time.
        Good luck.
Wait for the minibar.
        The first sad streaks of day's impure demise
dispersing worse light from the fallen skies
        cast all repinings into final shade
showing invisible truth as the unmade.
        Gold and then bronze expiring in the west
gave one more wrong turn to the evil wheel
        putting their quailing mettles to the test
on precious brasses no good thief would steal.
        Night glowing firily lit up its darks
of burning carbon blackest at the arc
        of total jet rejecting every ray

The Unconditional

towing dejection back into its black
        compacted vegetable heart of stone.
Told into epochs of compression which
        hold and then press down into precious dark
every least fibre over which we weep
        stark as the sleep I lose inside to win
in a 'lint-innerness' betrayed in grin
        coal waits interminably in the ground
known before any glance may ever strike
        each single facet slipping from its like
never retrieved from secrecy until
        infinishable as projections still
nor lit with less flame than the vinyl shelf
        of the perennially open overstore
blaring all signatures of total light
        like mere components of a final white
immortal amaranth above decay
        erasing lifespans from nocturnal day
whose emblematic vegetables gape
        a monopolychromatic subscape.
Dismantling deftly the one lit bulb left
        J turned his face In purest *Schwärmerei*
out to the darker Place of air where I
        watched his train winding With receding track

seeking nor finding ought To bring him back
        Night whose invisible Refusal paints
desire more feelingly Than visible taints
        impurest recollection of one bliss
still best remembered as the future hiss
        of slight retraction of the ceiling sky
in this experience of watching paint dry:
        First from a recent blurt of gesture out
smashing across a wall its several shout
        or then more moderately speaking through
its conversational andantes too
        whose swelling cadences crescendoed till
their speeches or their sermons in that rill
        echoed an era purposively lost
of thought in draperies more real than lost
        where at last grunts and whispers closed the scene
with blanker periods than could be seen
        meaning the slightest feathering of wall
or breath of colour on its roughened pall
        infinitesimally peaks and troughs
by nanometres were lit or switched off
        beneath the mindless sweep of human hand
leaving their tide withdrawing on the sand
        whose lakes and rivulets across a map

The Unconditional

of the whole plastered wall sat like a trap
        topography which needs must be of hell
since of no founded city speaking well
        demon metropolisses blistered up
the liquid pools of colour as a cup
        intensest concentrations of lost souls
thronging like fun in paint filled gaps and holes
        stuck in the ditch of a relief chart where
invented real wars lurch to prepare
        defective stanzas and their harshest lines
botched like the exclamation mark which whines
        at close of some rebelling poetries which hymn
all famous victories in counter-verse—
        I burns the bloody fioritura off
with purest flourishes against a doff
        whose maxi low low slowmos from its plot
as pomo twitters from a feline grot—
        or otherwhere some glimpse of wall showed out
from through the wall of colour blocking out
        the best white heaven of the colours through
imperfect screens of International Blue.
        Or rather when into a cloudless day
burning the green grass brown and then to grey
        a single blob of rain drops on a face

The Unconditional

waking the dust out from its novel trace
        and there already in its singleness
imparting news of all that comes to less
        and thus more like rain than the long rain storm
redundantly repeating every form
        so when the stream of paint made one least shrink
pulling its surface from the liquid drink
        into a tighter epitome of hue
then a quick blink of light lit up and through
        from off the happy surfaces of light
glowing as fiercely as the darkest night
        with whole anticipation of a drop
waiting to fall from the tight petal's top
        like a calm seventh hoping nothing less
from infinite protraction of its poise
        relaxed and tense expecting living truth
than domination to release no less
        than the whole flood of real happiness
so the first note of drying set the tone
        for what swift whistles then shrill or alone
gather to desiccant chorusses of stuff
        clustering dumbly to their shrieked enough
or more than nothing blinking from the wall
        in bacchanals of slightly less than all:

The Unconditional

or as when preparation rumbles round
        in repetitions to the same new ground
waiting to let the same tune hit the air
        as hit it last time from the same first fair
opens a bottle smashing at the neck
        enjoying right away the solo cheque
bounced up to paradise from endless debt
        both bliss and consolation for its loss
in double wrongness careless of the cost
        dismissing budgets of resentment which
sneer from both columns with a numbered itch
        and hot to boil down figures to the line
nor let one letter live that is not mine
        dealing instead of excrements in truth
of leavings left out from their remnant proof
        however glinting from the drying bed
ever again in blue bring out the red
        fresh as the haemoglobin to a cut
rips from the inside to the outside but
        endless recutting scores the single line
sung from the start to finish like no sign
        having no body which it is not first
vomit all goodness from your heart or burst
        or from a gut the better content comes

The Unconditional

more true the more it lacks those *if*s and *some*s
        inimical to every abstract might
tricked in the thinnest possible of nights
        run down the pigment alleys with a snort
under the blandest banners of an ought
        never receding from its virid no
forever joyfully negating so
        oriflammes lustrously bemoaning all
real recollections of untimely fall
        expecting muses to wind up their tops
vexed with mechanic music from the fops
        except too tuneless from the woundup stops
repeat or plink a cadence when it pops
        green as a tide ejected from the box
revenged on culture with a single pox
        electing antiperistalsis where
eventual being gives to nix that share
        no plenitude may lose but lose its self.
Rules of that drying form and founder down
        each moment that a single beam confounds
the varied but too stupid dumb surprise
        set up to please all undemanding eyes.
Wake up mate.
        Day dropping heavily into his lap

The Unconditional

pulled up prosthetic memories of task
        out to a tugged look over fleeting rail
whose half curve hardly oriented his
        quarter new sentience before all this
jumped from a tunnel to present a wall
        of half tall buildings clustered like a line
writing a profile on receding sky
        with too decipherable signature
made of their outlines on presumptive blanks
        then further detailed by the walls of eyes
built in a grid of serried windows' blinks
        in one squat foreground black while others' pink
or pyramidical grey tapers stood
        in each case no more separate from face
than any punctuated surface is
        immonsterably humanated which
asseverates its thousand eyed brick peach
        into the proposition of a name
scribbled across the donor of a theme
        just as a grille is never meant to smile
or scowl more than a helpless warping part
        so making dries into production when
its facial meanings mean more than a grin
        lacking the holy will of agent three

The Unconditional

to translate rage of metal from its glee.
        It just turned out like that.
Cheap plus the angles rock.
        All the characters are male.
Most characters have no character at all.
        Where homosocial cigarillos burn
all wit must strike the hour and take its turn:
        or heterously tow the other's line
greenly as grey can mirror kiss your mine.)
        in time to stop the chest and shoulders' fall
or tumble into richest rotting fruit
        ivied with contemplation's parasites
until they crest the last light on the brow
        shaping like ink upon the dark sky's page
blotting a glimmer from that fading stage
        where the brown lime trees shadow with their wood
all the bright matters spoken of for good.
        When at first light or rather 9.15
the dippy train emerged into the air
        blinking and too hung over into glades
they then meandered over like a stream
        of falsely deferential super-Is
clustering into twos and threes of chat
        ambling unpleasurably on the path

The Unconditional

in simulated leisure wearing mask
        grown to the formula of skin it bore
just as real needs demand the false one more.
        One serious thought stands single in that light
of the day's reveries in promenade.
        One stone I shall conduct you to could tell
the coldest chronicle of all that time.
        Qnuxmuxkyl, Fairless, Agramant and Smith
strode rapidly without the least idea
        of all itinerary in the walking van
denting the broad mud with their shod dispatch
        while Sacharissa Biedermeier trod
less speedily but with a clipboard there
        as Armstrong, =x. and Somerville tagged on
while single Jobless lingered at the back.
        The politics of gardening were explained.
The tout ensemble was an emblem tour
        in which chief patrons of the country good
one by one whitely pointed to the good
        now helpless that sole message to declare
without redoubled commentitious glare
        of the new gloss which made those stones work twice
once with their old and once with new presage
        of their long tenure in that softest page

in the rich catalogue where they may rest
        "limned" by the literal allegoregogue
and brought to silence with their country's best.
        It is the active left.
Kazoo composite.
        Agramant there had on his skulking cap.
Far down the food chain, slightly out of breath,
        attempting simpers at the wrong returns
of the dropped ball of conversation he
        half-housetrained tried to be polite but still
hit the wrong note by ignorance or skill.
        Qnuxmuxkyl striding half a pace too far
yet not so far to stop with proper wax
        the talk of discourses and of their shifts
which floated forwards in soprano tones
        re-representing non-discursive moans
of suffering workers reforgotten there
        signalled his breathing irritation then to Smith
with an abbreviated snort of air
        pushed through the nostrils with an equine burst
(distinguished nasal grimacing d'antan)
        and a quick glance which met the other's eye
caught in the snowfall of a little laugh
        cold as the Anglo-thinness of Smith's prose

The Unconditional

or chill as variants only Tanselle knows
        which checked Q's inner gratulation there
as he at once remembered the review
        which Smith had written of his monograph
cooling with faintness every lukewarm praise
        checking with anal pursings every fact
discovering no errors but two points
        of under-inking in the indexed tracts
and seeing personed in that blue-grey eye
        the same malicious shade of narrow I
which governed every clause before the "think"
        or verbal misnomer for scholar-sink.
Smith knew at once what this averted frown
        might be adverting to and stiffened up
preparing inwardly some sentences
        about the sterling contribution made
by Biedermeier's earlier work at least
        in refutation of Q's previous snort
before he could deliver ought of which
        by Fairless judging marvellous the whole
quite wonderful event and how the tea
        had been quite splendid with inanity
the scene was closed since they had reached a halt
        marked by some cupids pissing into salt

The Unconditional

or coarser rubble in a slimy bowl
      which =x. saw winking only at the top
of the long small ascent they dawdled up
      then saw them disappear across the lip
of visible matter to some other place.
      Lulled into dumbness by the dulcet drone
of speaking icons from the cicerone
      he dreamt as Armstrong busily took notes
while Somerville kept looking at his watch.
      Some yards behind him a clear imbecile
was shambling, dribbling, singing, muttering
      a flow of sounds which disconcerted =x.
by throwing up from time to time some phrase
      of greater eloquence than he had heard
for days or weeks or truthfully at all
      slobber with fearful beauty in its call.
They had been stood five minutes in the face
      of a stone gentleperson in his place.
Minute relation of what then was said
      only disgusts the reader too and me.
The grand dilapidations' wordless stare
      was born to waste its vacancy on air
and did so finely at each loss of edge
      complete that destiny in candid moss

The Unconditional

whose understated elegies of green
        said by not saying what those blocks might mean
more than the sluice's canopy of sedge.
        Thou hast brought me forth.
Perfect complacency was on the turn
        between its various senses in that smile
like bioluminescent photoforms
        mixing their languages from l to g
cold seeps and hot springs shelter there
        blocking h/er access to transcendence there
as Sacharissa sensed then that not all
        of all her party were in earshot there
and at the very instant when $=x.$ looked
        uphill to see the others disappear
she saw as he did not Q half glance back
        and almost meet her eye before he turned
away and vanished over the dark brow
        and she with inner half contempt and love
resume the history of Godfrey Dove.
        Then it was over. The half splashing tread
resumed its round of treat work for the head.
        When they at last arrived up at the top
of that slow incline all that met them was
        the same incontinent love gods who still

dribbled refusal of the Excise Bill.
        Had Q gone left towards the Rebel's Grot?
Or oppositely to that grassy spot
        amenably located at the foot
of sheltering banks whereunder cooling streams
        gave you five minutes' rest from wider themes
save for one scarcely noticeable jet
        remonitory graven finger set?
Jobless was fast approaching up the hill.
        Quickly they set off led by Somerville
in some direction so as not to let
        that deviant rhetor spoil the whole event.
Right out to eastern obsequies the trail
        lengthened before them as they briskly stepped
away from J who puffed up to the ridge
        looking to left and right to see no sign
of anyone except the coward flash
        of Armstrong's trainers and their distant plash
at which in *Resignation* he sat down
        ("Know anything specific on 'Resignation'"?
"Know anything resigned on 'Specificity'"?)
        signing his trousers with a greenish line
of cupid-droppings from the golded bowl.
        He looked back down across the prospect there.

The Unconditional

Unable to assimilate the least
        potential pixel into any scene
his face disorganized the whole machine
        staring back inwards into silent blanks
and lastly slumbering upon those banks.
        Ten seconds later he awoke in pain.
Grey as intelligible characters
        surfaces settled on the afternoon
and prophesying with a lonely drop
        rainstorms of all experience to wash down
across what marbled pedagogic frown
        a warm half breath off of the chalky down
sang through his lazy ear a vernal ode
        as J blinked round him looking for a map
and stumbled into more striated rock
        losing his eyeline to the path above
drifting then wandering downwards to a hole
        where a less deafened tympanum had rung
with what unknowing hearkening could sing
        in a whole shape of undetermined sound
either a human squawk or metal ground
        on metal squeaking like an infant cry
never already always known thus why
        and in a white allure of cannot tell

The Unconditional

strike up and out upon a passing bell
        irradiating pure noise from outside
(angelic messageless then not to be described
        in Klein text bottle with its small dumb seal
aslump nosidedness of I-won't-feel
        or I-won't-out-side of this happy gate
(a noise whose perfect purity remained
        as perfect emptiness of meaning chained
to pure possession of significance
        long after all phenomena renamed
whistled or beckoned by their master back
        to autodisambiguate from black
(preserved in absolute by vanishing
        from all interpretation of a thing
while J forever with a blip surmise
        whether from human pain or engine cries
listens to pure noise from a cloudy eye
        turned to all indecipherable colour I
step permanently out into the street
        eternally preconscious of a fleet
dispersing quietness along the path
        and breathing good air of the aftermath
in the first sand grain of a new rain shower
        or first subsecond of a finite hour

The Unconditional

take one correct gulp of a holiday
        secure at least from one misprision's sway—
from whose wrong absolute I cannot wake
        more than L-Language can be what there is.
(Life without language still must know it is.
        Language without life is its business suit.
The microcoat of transcendental lies.)—
        from whose wrong absolute I cannot wake
more than all these I cannot move an inch
        from this sole gap stopping a move or flinch
to any other order which is here.
        Where repetition is what in exists.
(Which prayer wheel I roll on and betray
        (I roll it on? so then much rather say
the wind breathes lungfuls of a gentleness—
        "Since it is said so widely that I live
how may I not confirm with every word
        that diagnosis of still breathing as
I write towards this reliquary of ink?" "Or hors commerce binbag anyhow."—
        it turns at any rate and weakly when
my every word is hatred to my friend
        and my success is only in his loss
and all my hope is that he be forgot
        and only I remembered in some tomb

The Unconditional

or other whose inaugural and lost
    first earthly purpose was to keep alive
against some day or other when all that
    reverse accounting would be justly done
or just done by some god or silent son).
    As "lack of cash" returns to "face I smash",
then to the bosom of that after church
    I cannot bear, yet cannot bear to leave.
Total transcendence furs its desert good.
    Only inhuman rock may now resist
ideal billows that would first prefer
    to rot the soulless soul-piece stuck inside
and paint its values in the desert sky.
    Let values then sing all our dearest cares
since values best know where the empty lie.
    Then values best can sing our dearest cares
since all immortal values never die.
    Choke on dry dust you must ever to hope
for what dust might refresh you and retrieve
    the image of that liquidable lie.
The whited bliss requires perpetual winter.
    As anchorets secure their bishoprics
my merry miserable auto purrs
    with inner life whose melancholic-lux

The Unconditional

so purples me to perfect ill I gape,
        renounce, renounce renouncing, motor on
through England's garland of internal organs.
        (Content de son naufrage he hardly feels
in any detail any grievous loss
        until the doorlatch trips his total up
by saying This and This to that serene
        first alibi that writes off every sharp
distress. Since when the bolshie metal clicked
        and just set off that time that that Mme
Guyon with half a smile of half half-sentience looked
        and made him think that shipwreck was not so
desirable as all that after all
        and him ridiculous with the fennel-
(up)-on his silly head in dignity
        (Then conversely a fallen hum of
sinistered dark strings oershadows every step
        say 1943 the initial drums
could hardly more emphatically explode
        had they designedly been mimicking
the pain inflicted on the subject field
        because when any artist gives the law
to him or Herself then the unfortunate
        who wait around will certainly have lots

The Unconditional

of opportunities to hear the drum
        hit loud as may be in the cause of truth:
oh cosmos, orchestra, the velvet I
        deliriously misincarnadine
a fist or finger painted like a sign
        which childishly gives up its skin to this
Old Germany or Ur-alt Mythkeller!
        Furtwängler! Rrrumbles-on; The sold slowed soul
(lesson: glow, long day, "viol", Ong)))
        so protest at a suffering I inflict
can barely register except as glee
        "wheree'er" I fail to occupy its hole
myself as the own criminal who shines
        in every worst behest I give, who cannot say
There is a world elsewhere and exit left
        nor who can ever direct debiting
pray without ceasing at the shrine of death
        for that we pray, we live; and that we live, we eat;
so that we eat we work and so we cease
        or so Yes Yes to complimentary creams
Yes Yes to stipend, Yes to purple themes
        the necessary footnotes to whose work
without all cynicism I may say
        appear in those accounts you may not see

unless by diligent research you find
        what few have ever cared to know or hope
(lay song low! long, Davy, oh long!)
        or ere some dictionary will provide
the stupid secret lacking an inside.
        "We are not obliged in every singular point.
Actual devotion cannot swallow up
        all time and care. Go on, you deserve
Not in a natural but moral sense
        we are broken by the immeasurable command.
Study to be quiet and do your job.
        Fastidious and drowsy listlessness
know is the absolute opposite of it
        Know naughty sloth or bad sequestering
is senseless indifferency in the place of it.
        We never can really love our neighbour.
Part sweetens the rest.
        Cyprian was liberal by wholesale, we"
fall down in royal parks and go to jail
        or Salome in the Italian cist
woven by parchment to the sainted list
        as knights hospitaller visited by girl
begging to be dug up out of the mud
        whose 'little heart' beneath the filbert tree

The Unconditional

invented first and then translated flies
        into the roomy martyrologies
to which fond rescues in these later days
        succeeds demystified reburial
since higher criticism hides them all
        where lower grubbers never may expose
so dogs and divers still avert the nose
        from any battered lump of happiness
redigging only where they must find less
        avenging desperadoes walking free
personifying rationality.
        Arriving backwards on a donkey first
gleefully drinking all the mud thrown up
        in sign of poverty which quickly turns
incorporating and annexing here
        transfigured in a talisman he wears
confounding all the merely fallen muck
        which sits about the false renouncer's neck
distinguished from *his* shining artefact
        as shit from spirit, ownership from use
whose famous miracles of killing well
        are passed down to a lethal wholemeal smile
having the power to wound and doing none
        again and over in crestfallen face.

But presto, let him live just as he will.
        "Want what you can, not what you cannot have.
Choose what is given from the datatray."
        Happy is that life which if we don't love
we do not have it.
        Use enjoys nothing at all.
"Two churches" still from firebombed caves can squeak.
        "One church, one sin" is all the good bombs speak.—
from finalized identity with loss
        since from that breathing street float without loss
pandifferential indiscernibles
        resisting message-messageless unbells
whom they dissolve insolubly in air
        ring from their inner atoms into air
and take the day off from the uniclock
        or write in palate clicks How To Unlock.)))
stationing happy J in lasting doubt
        and well hoped knowledge of the right way out.
Warm sun fell on his cheek.
        Free from capacity to will to move.
Unable as a rhizome to reflect
        his pink chin gazes off across the lawn
and shoe pips up upon the gravel walk
        as like obsidian as groan to groan

pointing with brainless digit to a branch
        of leaves which slightly waving in the air
failed quickly to be perfectly alike
        indifferentiably various
retraced from point to point their sole
        trajectories across the rended air
over whose tenderable needless shade
        J caught recurrently one flash of pink
or salmonated brick clashing with ought
        of managed marble sputtering its text
where bull and cricket, frog and bird and snake
        given no outlook but the junk we make
first gave to nought their look and then to things
        gave back a blankness as of all made things
whose pale pretended colour in that brick
        restored authentic thinness to what thick
prepatrimonially encrusted crud
        clogged up the book with estimable mud
and properly with alienable glint
        removed its alibi in one good hint
by gaping-Jobless as he stared prefixed
        taken with thinking pimples of his skin.
In his breast pocket an old photograph
        sat unregarded nor remembered too

staring its hardest at the linen bar
>over the skin and fat were shielding that
remembering muscle pounding out and back
>and fixed hat heartfelt pulse with frozen stare
harsh with the glitter of its noncompare
>where two or parallels or asymptotes
reflective only of whatever light
>traversed that square invariant in grey
paler than battleships but darker than
>an off white work shirt from the top left down
to some four centimetres from the top
>of the right side of that boxed section cut
out by the lens from some made chunk of stuff
>and kept a shadow nearly black between
their nearly silver strips of metalled sheen
>where on the left J now recalled three bands
of what must be some image mirrored there
>in one wide and two narrow blocks of shift
in bright or dark of aluminium stripe
>or on fools' aluminium aureate
with some transitional ambivalent
>thin passeggiatas of the change in hue
almost persuasive of that grey to blue
>as J gazed blankly wrapped into the sky

The Unconditional

scarcely believing what he saw or why
        the whole cold limit of his swimming eye
took one and perfectly reducible
        identical in Grey to that light patch
reading its image on that paper patch
        whose utter referencelessness made him snatch
for a missed beat inside the muscle-song.
        These and just these signs just adjust his throat
striking without an accident each note
        vented in duel with the woody song
of silent matter in resounding throng.
        This is the marble which I promised you.
Alone, utterly alone, in all that park
        the weeping emblem works a stony lung
barely more human than seraphic bark
        nor more angelic than a canine tongue.
Beneath a tomb like Clowdisley Shovell's
        or beneath tomb of Clowdisley Shovell stands
a breathing puttoplinth in unemployed
        sole instance of a sentimental droid
bleating his single ode out into print
        until one edge of fervour make a flinch
and give permissions to the optic nerve
        to grant cognizance of the largo swerve

The Unconditional

taken by one small blur of colour in
        the top left corner of the field within
and at that instant or then just before
        to hear the tone like mingled flutes and drums
whose querulous alarums of concern
        flutter with show of panic at the hums
of blatant nonsense they could now discern
        pushing them then as swiftly off away
and down behind another ridge of trees
        averting senses from the sign of death
they half heard squeaking in that shovel breath
        drowning its jouissant expiring cries
with critical perspectives on his eyes.
        Yet one in anamnesis shivered blest:
"It is no wonder if with froth and scum
        fervent renouncers bubble into view
since such saint-authors most of all asquint
        rusting in public with the russet few
scorn to confine that spirit to a box
        or learn home dialects of twofold knocks
putting themselves at distance from themselves
        with the grand artifice of bigotry
pinned to a spectre, staring at own zeal
        internally deflected from the true

standard of all assay or how to feel
        since no such hermits ever are alone
nor can such spirits ever leave their bone
        more than demonic echelons depart
the silverated innerworst of heart.
        There are doors enough to go out of life.
Somehow though they sit still where they are.
        Consider him whom lately now we saw.
The ancients saw their faces, but we can't.
        He hates his mirror and for this he bursts
these higher fluids out into the air
        hoping by deviation to go straight
to an inalienable bliss he thinks
        to seal up in a pamphlet or in pinks."
"What's this but hating our own faces?
        A verse self injury cut out upon
my arm or heart and last of all my tongue
        pleads for a help I will not stoop to ask.
I 'rather bleed to death' than 'doff my mask'."
        "His corrugated surface merely holds
a medium of disturbance between him
        and any hard word naming all his sin.
Whose ebbs and tides, his harsh versuras are
        no more nor less than gases from that star.

The Unconditional

Whose *Avant Satan!* leaking from the page
        speaks more the coward than of noble rage
and freshened into cloying atmosphere
        sprays an exotic-fruitage far and near
stopping the public nose with endless sweets
        or stuffing nostrils with their menthol treats
convert to candy every lump of shit
        by adding willpower to the dirty bit
I then ingest the second time for real
        rid of its sugar coating of I-feel
reciting backwards all that list of sins
        stamped out in panic lines across what skins
I ever hope to wear upon my skull
        content bone headedly to wrap me dull.
Look over there now where he stalks and grunts.
        Interminable preparation winds
or bludgeons to its heavy dominant
        so valses folles we voraciously await
already semaphore their would-be-mad
        over long plateaux of the just plain bad.
Suppress the resverys I ever knew
        with all the ones I never thought of too
while you and I shall hear him hit too hard
        the long drum solo of his self-regard."

The Unconditional

The other nodded gravely. They proceed
        in a held silence down the painted glebe.
Oxen moaned out their labours for a song
        impossible to tell apart from wrong.
"All whom I wished to please are in the grave."
        "Because you would not please them while they lived.
First moved to music by a slow demise
        you first desired and then bewept those ends
salting your pleasures down with loss of theirs.
        Friendless now sup up brick dust or choke best
of living stones the stumm mellifluousest.
        Just listen to your tuneless growl."
White out like the stuff scraped in top notes
        Of pitchblende or I can switch up in
Mischt part pixel of a grey heart swung
        Thin line of barium sulphate on the tongue
You did not notice anything
        Unusual or brush me with pale charcoal
You did not or on the subject
        I then mix up for my low tea drunk
Or I think and I gape and I broke
        By lose one get one I I can or
I name own nothing or I not form
        White as the skin sugar cut off it

The Unconditional

White or as the impossible the
        High or the keyless waves aired in the
Sky of a proposed hm extension
        Odalisk of my own back
Iron foliage is down
        Why or wrong whole image drown
Then I am or risk black sound
        I or am cut and brisk to a sole
Counterturn Now I slow round or so
        To whom I owe
Reliure-djinns gilding rules or carpeting, soft
        Then to go
Rule-uttering mock gliding I may drop
        3 Panblisterable miserable or I ha ha ve like a ha mm out
3a Scuppered lip tug or pup pule ha ve vee
        3c Puppered tip plug or zip yule me mee
d Ilionesk from doubt
        x To half half it
Darkening trebles the force of a top mmph tremble I cop
        Deafening all insentient source emblems where I stop
Down or off semblantly to tense more travellings when I will drop
        Daft it to halve or then I distribute with a fall cup
Exaninanimated from a purposed slip
        Fold the tip

The Unconditional

I can't
> Or hope lip

Me want
> Expredeterminated off that

Or exit
> Por exist

Rule and line
> Which I parole and I rope or lure in and I pore in or line

Soap
> Broken best then first open to a blood bit musical

Or adventitious stroke and eye dusvisual tele
> How I vent broke test or pick open a silly

Sent and made up by misspent fiction
> Prevented by thick shade of up in

As verveines sear or preserve delic-
> I ate the wrong bit or indelicate

Witch rediviva chariot me
> To white good by way of that old star

Which red or evil charivari
> To whit food by a way of that old

White or a wit or wait in a a
> Quite out of a partible x x

Incontingencies with your singu-
> Penalties lar or house gods hold off

The Unconditional

Interinanimating on no
        Inter in an in or in no out
Then I may
        Infer term in innerness que senefie
Inundate or soar sub as of sky counter-Chevrolet
        Maurizio Fantastic
In ondes or of martinet can swivel like zoo-wop through successive heavens
        Undine or an undying submarine announces the next episode and temple of Neptune
Anodynes of subaquatic dune prepare now
        Undrink me here
Under the aquamarine or marine green or over the marine sand your unseen dra-
    Ughts
Uvular or a velar unravel here are available or to reveal
        V-Disc Wartime Concert Paraphrase of Song of the Soldiers of the Sea (transc
J Magic Deadfinger Gimpel) transc Bren Sweett-Trolley) transc
        Push up an envelope or envelop in a hush P
Prayerwheel of the sheer phoneme
        Blocked off on my lip in pocks
Hcked as it were an ejective or expectorated or an unselectable
        Reject as it swerve in an unelective verve or an impermissible c-
Urve or Tove stood at the coastal bar or rob in my obsolete yearning episode again
        Whose waters are dark not only with their own but also with
Additional increments of absence and harsh remnant of the car scene
        Nor off any illuminable surface cark or rip up any part of a class or star

The Unconditional

Nor not cough off any ineradicable sourface hark or trip up any mart of a
        Ugh nor not not
As loss marks out its proposed fatefulness with a little detonation
        So fear extends its realm with a little deception
As the skin shrinks from its known tormentor
        So my each tongue muscle jumps with a little indirection
Up as the throat gulps up the proposed plug choke masquerades
        As indifference salves painless with a little less indecision
As in the end of deference referring its slaves with less of a little incision
        As an unending vale of suffering shedding allegory with a little inattention
As in an undated marvel or a laved trove bleeding mythful goth with a lot of flotation
        Or the tremendous rattle of ten thousand workers with banjos strikes out in a deafening
Collective harmony the impossible proposed perfectibility of mass
        Culture or any other culturalistic spectre or as another classificatory sector
Support with its revenue a clean room for a little phonetician
        Or other representative of best practice
So the lab claws
        And I balk
At the passionate nub of incapacity
        Barking with all knowledge
Privately printed
        Pay for my own lunch thanks
Says Poor proud pop perdu pro-parvenu
        Preselect as it were in an impermissible fricative

The Unconditional

Viral or store without rancour
        Veiling the dit-innervated devolved version of own rival
Formal bore doff that head in a repayment gesture made with one nostril with
        Better intelligence than ever wagged from your poor printout
Sent or collected urn hunches
        Then
I poem of D. Duck packed to the most with unpopular culture and trapp-
        I report on slowch slouch around three blocks in No Yo and then
I hot-houseboat it ProCelebrity Light Verse Hour-wards
        ł check in ł complete my expenses claim
Swiftly I shrivel at the thought of dog
        English boat
Inform twice > zero and twice > zero again dull mite-tray
        Then I can say
Sorry I had to write *Gurrelieder*
        Or say the limousine purrs like all yellowing paperb-
Black on its native gravel with a growl
        Brown nodding horrors of the teatime salvator
Back from a promenade not en velo but on v velour
        Autumnally as all auburn machinal and burning au leaf
Can it or press to rich money leaking all vinous nose notes
        Can camp Campaspe or er I 'zgjh sdkj' then
Zemloyu
        I must

Zemblan rasp-
      You must bury
I eye or snout out a I why I
    ;¨¹3XFí(«X°°ëZøv☐ ¹ÿ☐ T2IéÅ|☐ ûe|P☐ ö¯☐☐☐ í2ÂÞlØ~3Ú½ÇãGÇ
Entire text of my fucking essay
    P
La
    Es
Ah
    Se
Ul
    Rt
Ee
    Sr
Oa
    Fn
Md
    Ia
Ns
    Oh
Ra
    Vd
Ei
    Rn

The Unconditional

Sg
        Ek-
kind of cool
        Interposition as a cloud
No
        Determiningly comprehend each most extended tongue of spirit in my
Dim yet still clarifying sound map as of all listening or dumb not deaf or glistening
        Determinately erase when what evasing vague areas of spiritlessness can or will claim
Disesperatively revive with vir or can cano of minute compassion this bashed up
        Diminishment of own soul sunken in the abashed lossface and its nerveless cheek
Dyspraxially to disprefix a a praxis or are that is one good
        Disincarnation not sliding aloft but singing open at open Love
Diminish my sin and magnify only what from you
        Deliver me and it all up
Or
        Disinter not this limp receptacle to that infallible efficacious grace
Rather I in am memberment of this entire frame known or dissolved through its/I blood
        Disinvest no proposed burnt sector for subsumpt
Dive rather for the whole imaginable loss and burn only the guarantee ticket
        Down among whatever catacombs among amounted to or drop dead
Only to not drown but breathe up rather as it were droppingly
        Dissevering from all pap pliable la labile lap wrappings of palp
Forever while it ever is perfectly distinct from whatever is dead
        Panirrelinquishible

The Unconditional

Or as of nevergeglaubt der du deliver no more than arrival
        Denounce disown and discard me while I still walk
Nowhere
        In particular
And only there
        Goodbye
Or goodbye bears my singularity
        and which I kill towards with every gain
hoping to make that moveless deathmask sing
        when merely thrown out with the rubbish where
a weak wind crossing it may draw such strains
        just as a first love literally tells
the characters without which you won't come
        to gem or skeleton of infinite
concretion known beforehand in their lines.
        Just as a category nears its own demise
by signalling with bells and whistles all
        its infinite validity across
the whole field open to it while its ink
        vehicularizes all the untruth sat
in its own skeleton of vehemence
        and thus negating like a parasite
the host whose hospitality it has
        so long enjoyed before refuting it:

The Unconditional

or as a human writes negation when
        wishing to translate torture into cash
so contradiction in the object may
        hoping determinately to resist
think its own woodenly true matters where
        now to six letters reason barks a Yes
while real oblivion snores a quiet No
        cathected fetishistically now
Powerless to break my head upon a stone
        Or coax blue fluid from an ageless bone
Turning my right hand over to my left
        Turning my left again to turn to right
Turning from wrong head to the one bereft
        Turning again from that loss to the light
Turning aside to turn towards the sun
        Turning around the still earth in a wish
Flattened against the wrong world told and done
        Turning from speaker to a tongueless dish
Flattened against the wrong light of the sun
        Turning against return into the lip
Flattened against the limit of the sky
        Turning the wrong way back into a lung
Flattened against the ocean floor or why
        Turning the metal pips against their sung

The Unconditional

Flattened inside a cubicle of fire
        Turning myself alone wherever I
Stand quite unable to remove a foot
        Turning too uselessly to lever my
Standstill away from stuck stood like a lump
        Turning to turn away from all when I
Changed out of mind and out of matter where
        Turning to innerwards may not repair
Changed into substance less by love or hate
        Turning to subject all my loveless state
Changed into subject less by serpentine
        Turning to substance all that is not mine
Must become audible without a cry
        Turning the volume down to zero or
Must become verbal wordlessly in my
        Turning the zero down from volume for
Must become human in my every claw
        Turning the talon inside-out to think
Must become sighted out of silvering
        Turning across the whole extent of land
Repeating turns however there erased
        Turning a small coin over in a hand
Repeating syllables where no amazed
        Turning to hear turns back to go to sleep

Repeating deafness of the inner ear
        Turning to cross out any thinking leap
Repeating prohibitions on the sheer
        Turning revertedly to maximum
Repeating truth of any true idea
        Repenting first at absolute despair
making this ninety-first the real start
        or end of absolute relinquishment
Wipe Frühlingssehnsucht
        Wipe Abschied
look in the mirror at my ugly face
        unable to detect the smallest love
in eyes more lifeless as the mobile tongue
        more wets the name of life around that hole
where every toxin comes both in and out
        caught in the act of looking like a nil
I from an accidental unpoliced
        corneal sector must receive as news
the relative autonomy of skin   *Anfang*
        put out of countenance by my own chin
crossing the frozen waste of Jobless' cheek   //
        whose pudding shadows with a languid dip
gently vibrated on a silvering   *Ausgang*
        stuck like the cellulose no stomach can

The Unconditional

turn into meaning with however harsh
        logistic bile brought up to summarize
the plenitude of infinitely same
        or terminable Difference which yawns
and therefore rather stared his gaze quite out
        with real refusal of construction there
or real refusal of refusal where
        the facial hair could never be erased
enough to let it from that look be saved
        hailed there forever by some lifting stuff
thinking its own thoughts of not quite enough
        or with a palpable declension shifts
away from all that glance's panic gifts
        I where an eye inserted owns its stump
me like an irrefigurable lump
        saving alike from plenitude and hell
impossibility of thinking well.
        To be is to be the value of a bound variable.
Stranded in my own fat reserves.
        Jobless moved frightened back towards the door
feeling one slip of air upon his face
        knowing this not to be unconscious gas
nor not to be impersonated breath
        but rather apophatically trod

The Unconditional

one scale away from music to the street
        ingesting all the quite unnameable
lungfuls of worse reality by gulps
        steadied by faltering where really weak:
strengthened in song by failing to a squeak:
        stripping by one and one all thought away:
thinking without reflection into day:
        thrown without reservation into grief
or melancholic into true relief
        ready to hear and answer any friend
crying from human proteins without end
        acknowledging each step along a road
of sentience which even yet remains.
        All this is not to say there is no dusk
when from a fatal strand the many leave
        a solitary gazer on the shore
in dry complicity with soaking gore
        a light hole cannot open in a cloud
dissevering forever with a gap
        a brief shape taken by the golden lap
of the sole figure made one minute since
        by that no fabric where no meaning glints.
A light skiff floats off under slight surmise
        leaving indifference for other skies.

The Unconditional

So may a single fragrance on the air
        summon some others which at once repair
communicatingly to utterance
        placing the stations of their unseen track
from break to breaker on the ocean's back
        to conjure thus the true and comic god
dropping his trident with a shrug or nod
        or non maestoso darting to recline
on those damp couches where the lobsters dine.
        Plenty crustaceans dancing à la grecque
whistle free beauty in an arabesque
        then saunter out quite quickly as the bill
drops on the seafloor from the mumbled krill
        detecting well whose subreptitious charms
you perhaps chasten from their leadingstrings
        all errant infant artists patters where
excess of nature spills out over their
        porpoiseless task too functionless with fish
gasping from gills which lip it on dry land
        evaporating with a helpless wish
refusing aid from any human hand.
        Cerise or cherry as a slip of air
coloured by distant gases and/or fair
        only by gaps or distanced middles who

The Unconditional

paint every oxygen with all untrue
        elaborated alibis of light
which foam up skywards where melodious night
        settles its word alone upon the brink
of limitation to the briny drink.
        Ten years later I stood at the long edge
of the same coastline darkened almost quite
        into invisibles I would colour north of black
hoping with an unmade hand gesture to declare the extent
        or as though by this act of nearly inert calmness the ageless
indiscernible limit turned from sand to the unfree repetition of sea
        sectionally in seven panels printed on silver gelatin and then sealed
across in a line from left to right leave indiscoverable
        the source of a light left glimmering over the immeasurable or if from Cimmerian
scarce rememberable terminus in its differential and uneven fade
        like what will be darkening for the last time in this one way autumnal.
In reconciled technologies of light as it falls
        ever on the eye whether from darkened room or from hand
I over inconspicuous ether or dead heather prefer
        what I as lilac or now grey or now purple may lately
where in a fiery brown no leaf appears
        or any other foliage than the reddest grass
from eyes given a light prepared by habituation to the dark
        both what records and what invents a line

reverting with what love
        not to the first but to some future recollection or unremembered
sweep or accurate descent
        right from the left edge to the sweetest far
corner of solitude where two red dots
        just mark the faint dark of a dim stopped car
beside whose outline I may just surmise
        the mail box at the road to Findlay Point.

        QNUXMUXKYL

While from that littoral the ships depart
        slipping their moorings for the thought of west
slow footfall eastward loses any art
        of recollecting any former best
since in its hopeless tread away from light
        no arc of playful lightness sweetens work
as a lit bark upon a glassy sea
        salts down with part of labour into night
what bears it up upon that surface strength.

        AGRAMANT

My spectre bends back to the groaning east.
        My emanation scarpers to the left.

The Unconditional

My bones awarded to the evil feast.
   My books and papers to the last man left.
My possibilities disperse in air
   or in its parallel equivalent
unbreathable innavigable yet
   choking with fluid absence living foes
from whose real ending I suck endless strength.

    =x
I walk back slowly from the seaside hut
   feeling each pressure in my foot at last
from the real ground of every reasoning
   which decorated with a proper top
of earth and grass and tarmac on its top
   renunciator of sheer givenness
I neither make my mirror nor my tomb
   nor neither-nor it in a darkened room.
I walk back slowly from the seaside hut.

    JOBLESS
Deil*i*ns.
   Iicd*n*k
Enpo*es*.

The Unconditional

        OaaneS
Frierj
        Aonaea
Rmwntr
        Oaedhv
Stlsai

        QNUXMUXKYL

While Lesquax yet eludes his waited end
        Tanagram boils sequentially his friend
or grammars tan their boss ile in the sun
        quailing at oil sex as the colours run
and wake up one day when a purple tie
        is all the neckwear in the rack then die
the morning planet not the evening star
        more than is equals equals on the far
diminishing horizon of a skin.

        AGRAMANT

I join no chorus; I pretend no love.
        My book is written and my bills are paid.
I seal up all my legacy in packs
        I rubberize against a fingerprint

The Unconditional

and label tersely first before I send
        some to a lasting name and some to dust.
Then I uncrease my fold or print of mind
        burning all sectors which might hanker back
to any taste of origin or end.

        =x

The surface of the water climbs and falls
        quite indisseverably from the thought
of feeling knowledge in a fingertip
        pressing against another and then back
where no pure eyelight can shed human air
        nor stare its mirror to a letter there
but rather drown to prove its sensing touch
        dies like all mortal thinking off a lip.
The surface of the water climbs and falls.

        JOBLESS

Mm
        nn
mm
        mmn
nnh

The Unconditional

        mmmc
c – mm
        m – c
m – c – m

        QNUXMUXKYL

The hour of feeling supplements a gap
      with too diverting stories from a tap
open by default or when closed by luck
      squeaking with wishes to relate or tuck
as episodes of ecstasy return
      inside the holding dwelling where they burn
too gently to disturb the sponsor's tent
      or give out any shriek as felt or meant
more than decaying particles are skin.
      A little arch; a grille of iron struts.
A glass; opaque; a frosted top; a bar.
      Soft; drop; soft, soft: sort or doff off, rough prop,
creep, crawl or limp; slough off or cough up a skin
      raw at imp pop or froth magnet
then more at him drop or put forth a step;

The Unconditional

        slow, slow: walking with no
load of return but loss: so if stop tops
            salt or another inefficacious substance
I may quake, quail or may awake
        backwards from hell;
I may put one foot
        I may have
behind
        another
so, so: with which learnt breathing
        data float down; the own rote load doles out
a doubt-loud flow into the overload.
        Facts, moping at their blindless diurn, tread
the light to dumb muck for cash in one line.
        Hush dim glut making a linear red.
Hush now to a mindless lucky smash.
        Infinitesimally aperture
the single seamless of the done told world
        or prise the top off the creep in one dull.
Then, last low vocative of the ending-cult,
        blow out the pilot light.
Empty this plea of efficacity.

)))))

NOTE

This poem is metrical. Readers may wish to give the character =x. a value equal to, or slightly smaller than, that of the name of the letter "s" (the symbol for indefinite stress) when spoken aloud. For purposes of performance, if any, the character could be rendered by so much of a gulp as can be achieved without swallowing.